Using
WRITING
PORTFOLIOS
To Enhance
Instruction And Assessment

by Marjorie Frank

Incentive Publications, Inc.
Nashville, Tennessee

Cover and illustrations by Kathleen Bullock
Edited by Jan Keeling

Library of Congress Catalog Card Number: 93-80014
ISBN 0-86530-281-2

PRINTED IN THE UNITED STATES OF AMERICA

TABLE OF CONTENTS

I. GETTING TO KNOW WRITING PORTFOLIOS

II. DEVELOPING AND USING WRITING PORTFOLIOS

III. EVALUATING WRITING PORTFOLIOS

IV. SOME FINAL ADVICE AND SAMPLE FORMS

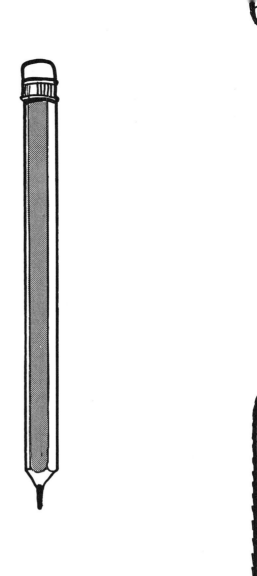

I. GETTING TO KNOW
WRITING PORTFOLIOS

The new assessment evaluates the process, not just the product.

Students and teachers become partners in writing assessment.

There's a revolution underway in the world of assessment. The whole concept of assessment is broadening and changing in some very exciting ways. Writing assessment has been strongly impacted by the changes—with benefits galore. Now, teachers and students can get a much better look at how students work with the writing process. On top of that, the new assessment techniques have the wonderful effects of improving writing skills, enhancing writing instruction and increasing students' excitement about writing.

WHAT'S HAPPENING?

The changes in assessment come out of an attempt to learn more about **how** a student learns. There is a lot of **watching** of students. They are observed as they actually **perform authentic** tasks. Thus, these are the two words most frequently used to describe this new assessment.

PERFORMANCE ASSESSMENT

Performance assessment means that the student performs the type of behavior that is being measured and the performance, not just the final product, is evaluated.

<u>Performance Assessment for Writing:</u> To assess writing ability or progress, the student is asked to write. Instead of checking to see if a student can choose correct sentences or answer questions about writing, writing assessment is based on the observation of how the student uses the writing process.

AUTHENTIC ASSESSMENT

The "new" assessment also strives to be as **authentic** as possible. This means that not only does the student perform the type of task being measured, but the student demonstrates the behavior in a situation as much like real life as possible. Authentic assessment has its basis in activities that are meaningful and interesting to the student. And authentic assessment involves the student in self-evaluation.

<u>Authentic Writing Assessment:</u> The student is asked to write on a topic of her choice and interest in a normal setting at her usual pace and timing, using the process ordinarily followed for classroom writing. Upon finishing the task, the student does some sort of self-reflection on the writing. If the writing is evaluated, the criteria for evaluation would be clear to the student before she writes.

A CLOSER LOOK AT STUDENT WRITING

The actual observation of students writing yields a much more in-depth view of what students are learning, how they're handling the writing process, and how they're growing.

- No longer is writing ability or progress determined by a focus on the end product.

- No more does the teacher face those mysteries about how students have arrived at the pieces of writing that are the end results.

- No longer is writing instruction separated from writing assessment.

And perhaps, best of all...

- No longer are students bystanders in the assessment of their own writing achievement.

NEW WRITING ASSESSMENT

- is ongoing

- gives students and teachers an inside look at how they write

- takes the emphasis off the product and puts it on the process

- shows a wide range of skills

- makes problems, strengths, needs apparent right away

- looks at writers and writing over a long period of time

- ties assessment to instruction

- makes students and teachers partners in writing assessment

- gets the students actively involved in self-assessment

- takes away the mysteries about what the writer is thinking

PORTFOLIO ASSESSMENT

Perhaps the most exciting piece of the assessment revolution is the use of portfolios for learning about student growth. In the field of writing, portfolios are especially workable and valuable for enhancing assessment and instruction.

WHAT IS IT?

Portfolio assessment is a process of evaluating student work, achievement, progress and/or attitudes on the basis of a collection of work done by the student.

This collection, representing efforts on a variety of tasks over a period of time and supplemented by student self-reflections, gives kinds of information that a teacher could never possibly gain through traditional methods.

Portfolios— perhaps the most exciting part of the assessment revolution.

The portfolio process is a natural for assessing the writing process.

PORTFOLIOS AND THE WRITING PROCESS

Portfolios are a natural evolution of the process approach to writing. Writing IS a process. The portfolio approach is also a process—one that beautifully emphasizes, encourages and assesses the writing process.

Furthermore, portfolios make it possible to get a unique and thorough look at how a student is **actually performing** the writing process.

The section of this book titled, **"Why Use Writing Portfolios?"** will elaborate on the many benefits that can result from using portfolios for writing instruction and assessment. And all of the book that follows is designed to help you create and use your own Writing Portfolio project to bring many of those benefits to your classroom.

MANY USES FOR PORTFOLIOS

The ways portfolios are used for assessment are almost as numerous as the users. All across the country, systems have been designed by states and school districts mandating portfolio use. In many more schools, teachers or groups of teachers are fashioning their own portfolio projects.

This book focuses on Writing Portfolios. You may design portfolios for writing only. Or writing may be a section of a language arts or multi-discipline portfolio. Whatever the subject, the writing processes and skills are a part of any portfolio process, because the all-important ingredient of self-reflection generally involves writing.

Later in this book a variety of uses for writing portfolios will be discussed. But the main message about portfolio use for writing or any subject is this: There is no one right way to use portfolios. Portfolio use depends entirely upon the purposes for their use and the needs of the students and the needs of the classroom.

There is no one right way to do portfolios.

Do your homework before you try portfolio assessment.

DO YOUR HOMEWORK

While there is no one best way to do portfolios, it is important to learn as much as you can before launching their use. Recent years have yielded a wealth of data, research and experience in portfolio assessment. The possibilities are wonderful. But the topic is not simple. And all portfolio assessment is not automatically good assessment.

If this is unfamiliar territory for you, do as much research as possible before you begin. That way, you'll gain the benefit of learning from the efforts and errors of others.

WHAT IS A WRITING PORTFOLIO?

Writing Portfolios don't just reward good writing— they help to make all writing good.

I make most of the selections.

DEFINITION

A **WRITING PORTFOLIO** is an organized and purposefully selected collection of work that shows the student's achievement, efforts, growth, and attitudes in the area of writing. The collection includes some statement or evidence of the portfolio purpose, reasons or criteria for selection of pieces and examples of student self-reflection on the work.

"MUSTS" FOR THE WRITING PORTFOLIO

- The student must be involved in the selection of the content.

- The purpose of the portfolio must be evident from looking at the portfolio.

- Samples selected must fit the purpose of the portfolio.

- The portfolio must include student self-reflection on some or all of the work.

- The portfolio must include samples that show growth.

- If the portfolio is used for assessment, it must include the criteria by which pieces and/or the whole portfolio will be evaluated, judged or graded.

A portfolio is a window into the writer's mind.

A writing portfolio is not just a collection of writing.

A portfolio is a moving picture of what the writer can do.

A WRITING PORTFOLIO IS NOT...

A Writing Portfolio is not just a random collection of writing.

It is not a folder of writing samples chosen and saved by the teacher.

The focus of the portfolio is not on individual writing assignments. A piece of writing is never done **for** the portfolio. The focus is always on the student—a living, growing writer and learner.

The portfolio is not a narrow or time-limited collection. It holds samples collected on several occasions over a period of time.

A portfolio is not static. Anything can be changed, revised or replaced. A student is never held back or labeled by a piece of writing.

The Writing Portfolio is not a thing that rewards only good writing. The portfolio process helps the writer to make all writing good.

The portfolio is not the sum of individual parts. A work of writing is not looked at in isolation from other pieces. Nor is it compared to others' writing. Each work is seen as one part of the whole on-going story of a writer's growth.

A WRITING PORTFOLIO TELLS A STORY

The portfolio tells a personal story of who the student is as a writer, a thinker, a learner. It is a window into the writer's mind. It follows the person over time and tells the story of the writer's successes, struggles, questions, change and growth. It is like a moving picture or a scrapbook of what the writer can do.

WHY USE WRITING PORTFOLIOS?

There are many benefits that come from using portfolios for writing. A wide range of good things can happen, supplying gains for the students, the teacher and other audiences such as parents and administrators.

WHAT STUDENTS GAIN

Writing Portfolios let students:

- own their own work

- develop independence as learners

- develop greater understanding of the writing process

- have choice in selecting

- take an active part in setting goals and making decisions

- learn to think about their writing

- learn to assess their own strengths and weaknesses and evaluate their own progress

- develop a fuller understanding of their abilities

- gain a greater appreciation of their growth and themselves

- think of themselves as writers

- feel free to take risks and try new approaches without risking a bad grade

- write better...write more...and enjoy it more

Portfolios get kids thinking of themselves as writers.

WHAT TEACHERS GAIN

Writing Portfolios give the teacher:

- a clearer view of student growth, interests, needs, achievement, difficulties, successes

- a multi-dimensional profile of the student as a writer

- a view of the strategies a student uses to generate writing topics and content

- insights about your writing instruction and quick feedback on instructional needs

- a great way to join writing assessment and instruction

- a look at student attitudes about writing

- insights into a writer's awareness of the writing process

- a more accurate way to pinpoint strengths and weaknesses

- clues about how a student handles a particular writing skill over time and in various settings

- a look at how a student's writing is changing over time

- a satisfying partnership with students in goal setting, decision making and evaluation

- a chance to discover who individual students really are

The teacher gets a multi-dimensional look inside the writer.

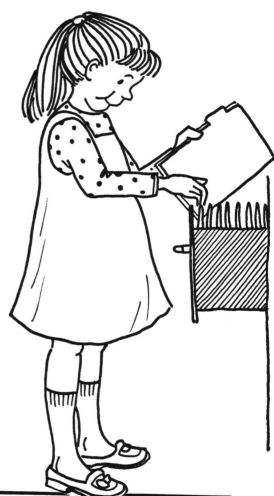

A writing portfolio is the portrait of the writer.

WHAT PARENTS GAIN

When included in the portfolio process, parents:

- see their child's progress first hand

- get a broader, deeper view of student growth

- see, appreciate and understand their child's strengths as a writer

- learn about the writing process

- learn how a person develops as a writer

- watch the writer's growth over time

- gain an appreciation for the instruction provided their child

- are invited to take part in the assessment of the their child's progress

- learn what authentic assessment is

- get a real and meaningful way to support their child's learning

WHAT ADMINISTRATORS GAIN

Portfolios can provide school personnel with:

- a pass-along record of student writing activities and growth

- a tool for showing what's going on in writing instruction

- a vehicle for collecting some wide-scale assessment data

Portfolio purposes must be based on students' needs.

DON'T
START
WITHOUT
A
PURPOSE

PURPOSES OF WRITING PORTFOLIOS

There is no **one** right purpose or set of purposes for using Writing Portfolios. The portfolio purposes are as varied as the projects that different schools or teachers design.

There are some key concepts to consider, however, when choosing purposes for your Writing Portfolio system:

1) The purpose is not to **do** Writing Portfolios. The purposes you choose will have, instead, to do with helping kids learn.

2) You need to decide the purposes before you begin portfolio use.

3) **All decisions** about purposes of the Writing Portfolio should be based on the needs of the students and the needs of your classroom.

4) You cannot determine the type, contents and use of the portfolios until you have decided upon the purposes.

5) Be open to the possibility that other purposes will come to light as you get involved in portfolio use.

So, if you are getting ready to use Writing Portfolios, deciding the purpose will be one of your first steps.

To get at your purposes, ask yourself:

What do I want to happen for students?

How will I know when it happens?

A SAMPLING OF PORTFOLIO PURPOSES

Writing Portfolios can be designed for use as instructional tools or as vehicles for writing assessment or both. Whatever the uses you intend, make sure the purposes are clear to teachers and students alike before you begin the portfolio process in the classroom.

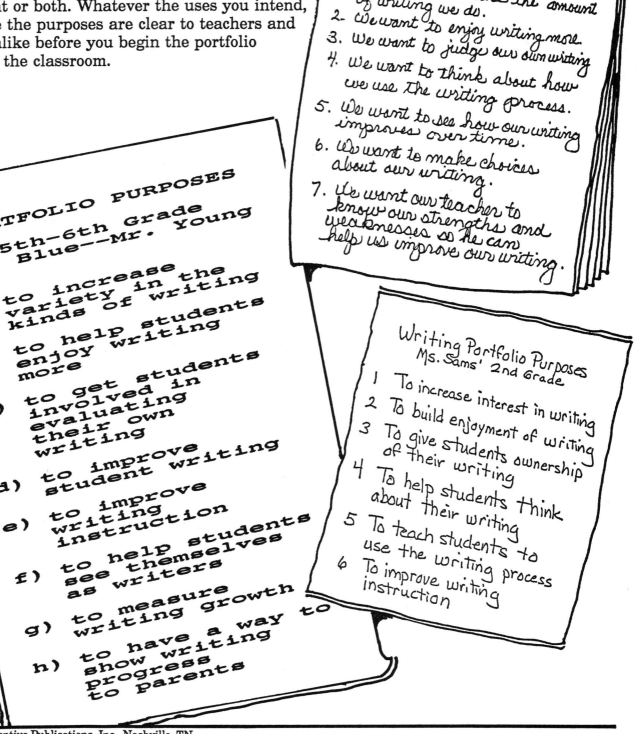

Purposes of Writing Portfolios
Mr. Yng's 7th gr Eng.

1. We want to increase the amount of writing we do.
2. We want to enjoy writing more.
3. We want to judge our own writing
4. We want to think about how we use the writing process.
5. We want to see how our writing improves over time.
6. We want to make choices about our writing.
7. We want our teacher to know our strengths and weaknesses so he can help us improve our writing.

PORTFOLIO PURPOSES
5th–6th Grade
Ms. Blue—Mr. Young

a) to increase the variety in the kinds of writing
b) to help students enjoy writing more
c) to get students involved in evaluating their own writing
d) to improve student writing
e) to improve writing instruction
f) to help students see themselves as writers
g) to measure writing growth
h) to have a way to show writing progress to parents

Writing Portfolio Purposes
Ms. Sams' 2nd Grade

1. To increase interest in writing
2. To build enjoyment of writing
3. To give students ownership of their writing
4. To help students think about their writing
5. To teach students to use the writing process
6. To improve writing instruction

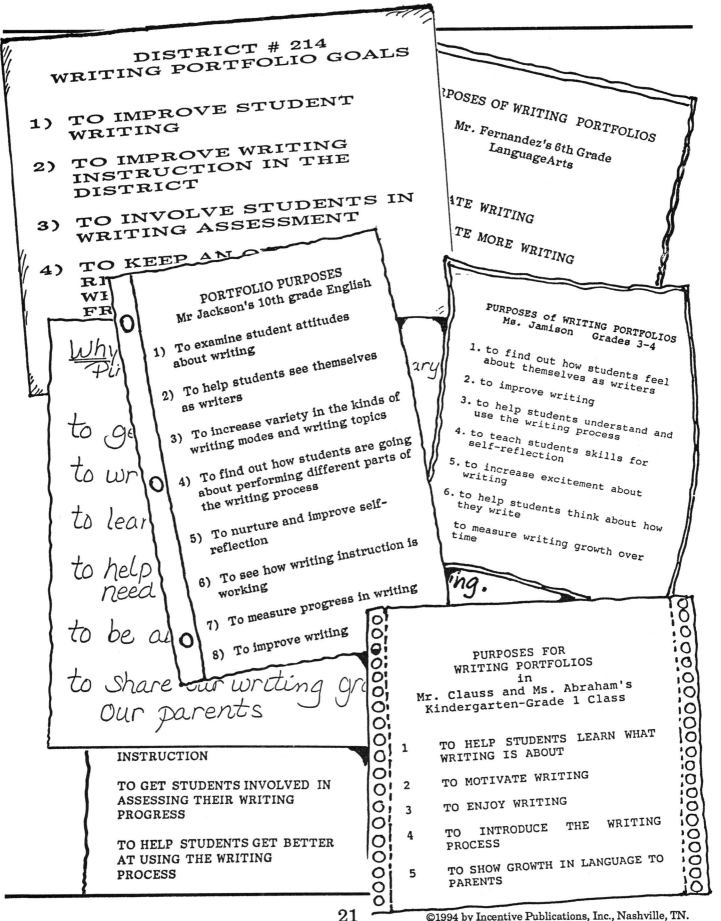

DISTRICT # 214
WRITING PORTFOLIO GOALS

1) TO IMPROVE STUDENT WRITING

2) TO IMPROVE WRITING INSTRUCTION IN THE DISTRICT

3) TO INVOLVE STUDENTS IN WRITING ASSESSMENT

4) TO KEEP AN O...
   R...
   WI...
   FR...

PURPOSES OF WRITING PORTFOLIOS
Mr. Fernandez's 6th Grade
LanguageArts

...TE WRITING

...TE MORE WRITING

PORTFOLIO PURPOSES
Mr Jackson's 10th grade English

1) To examine student attitudes about writing

2) To help students see themselves as writers

3) To increase variety in the kinds of writing modes and writing topics

4) To find out how students are going about performing different parts of the writing process

5) To nurture and improve self-reflection

6) To see how writing instruction is working

7) To measure progress in writing

8) To improve writing

PURPOSES of WRITING PORTFOLIOS
Ms. Jamison   Grades 3-4

1. to find out how students feel about themselves as writers

2. to improve writing

3. to help students understand and use the writing process

4. to teach students skills for self-reflection

5. to increase excitement about writing

6. to help students think about how they write

to measure writing growth over time

Why...
Pl...

to ge...

to wr...

to lear...

to help...
   need...

to be a...

to share our writing gr...
   our parents

INSTRUCTION

TO GET STUDENTS INVOLVED IN ASSESSING THEIR WRITING PROGRESS

TO HELP STUDENTS GET BETTER AT USING THE WRITING PROCESS

PURPOSES FOR
WRITING PORTFOLIOS
in
Mr. Clauss and Ms. Abraham's
Kindergarten-Grade 1 Class

1 TO HELP STUDENTS LEARN WHAT WRITING IS ABOUT

2 TO MOTIVATE WRITING

3 TO ENJOY WRITING

4 TO INTRODUCE THE WRITING PROCESS

5 TO SHOW GROWTH IN LANGUAGE TO PARENTS

WHO OWNS THE PORTFOLIO?

One of the first decisions that needs to be made about the Writing Portfolio is who owns it. Determining ownership is a major decision—one that has strong implications for the purposes, contents, processes, uses and benefits of the portfolios.

OWNERSHIP QUESTIONS

Portfolio ownership involves such questions as:

- Who decides what goes in it?—and what doesn't go in it?

- Who decides what the student writes to begin with?

- How is the portfolio handled?

- How and where is it stored?

- Who makes decisions about the portfolio processes?

- Who has access to it? Why?

- Who evaluates the portfolio?

- Are the contents private or public?

- What happens to it at the end of the year, semester or class?

My portfolio says, "This is who I am."

THE AUDIENCE MAKES A DIFFERENCE

In planning for portfolios, it is important to ask "Who are the audiences?" and "What will each one want to learn from the portfolios?" Students need to know up front who will have access to the contents. This will make a difference in their contributions and in what the portfolio shows.

It is also crucial to be aware of what is gained and lost with each addition of a group of readers. In general, the more "institutionalized" the portfolio becomes or the further ownership gets from the student and the classroom, the less likely it is that the portfolio can fully show who the student is and what the student's writing abilities really are.

A general principle to follow for all audiences is to allow the student to present or explain, in his or her own written or spoken words, the purpose and content of the portfolio.

PORTFOLIOS FOR DIFFERENT PURPOSES

One way to avoid the losses that occur when portfolios become more public is to design a portfolio flexible enough for different purposes. Students retain close ownership, privacy and control over who views their work on an ongoing basis throughout the year. But at specific times, they prepare the Writing Portfolio for viewing by a particular audience. At these times, they remove or add whatever they wish for that purpose.

If the portfolios are to be passed on to the next teacher or examined by district officials, the students can prepare a "Public" or "Pass Along" Portfolio that contains only the elements they want to have read by a wider audience.

The student must feel a strong sense of ownership of the portfolio.

STUDENTS—THE PRIMARY STAKEHOLDERS

In order for the Writing Portfolio to truly tell the personal story of a writer, the student must feel a strong sense of ownership. If the goal is to accurately reflect a student's abilities and growth and to involve students in self-assessment, then student ownership becomes even more crucial. Students must feel free to share personal thoughts and experiences and to include pieces of writing that show many sides of themselves. They must feel comfortable including honest self-evaluations of work and reflections on the portfolio process. This can only happen when students know that they have much control over the portfolio.

Of course, others, such as teachers and parents, have interests and roles in the portfolio process as well. It is unlikely that Writing Portfolios would fulfill their purposes in any classroom without guidance, instruction and input from someone else during portfolio development. And it is desirable for students to have responses to writing and to portfolios from peers, parents, teachers and others. However, the student must remain the primary owner in order for the portfolio to be the real story of that student.

There are many workable systems in which the teacher has some influence on portfolio processes while at the same time students enjoy the benefits and responsibilities of ownership. This happens in classrooms where teachers work carefully to build a partnership with students so that decisions about Writing Portfolios are made jointly.

WAYS TO PROMOTE STUDENT OWNERSHIP

Students feel ownership of their Writing Portfolios when they are allowed and encouraged to:

- create and design their own portfolios—inside and out

- choose writing assignments that are of interest and relevance to them

- have the major role in selecting what goes into the portfolio and what does not go into the portfolio

- have free and easy access to their portfolios

- take part in making decisions about how the portfolio system is going to work—design, contents, selection, organization, reflection, sharing, evaluation, criteria

- have a major say in who looks at the portfolio...and when

- view and respond to one another's portfolios respectfully and with permission

- contribute self-reflections

- participate in portfolio evaluation

- help set criteria for evaluations

- share the portfolio in ways they choose

- watch a teacher create, enjoy, value, and share his or her own portfolio

The less ownership I have, the less my portfolio tells my story.

OTHER STAKEHOLDERS

Anyone who has an interest in the student's learning and who, therefore, may desire some access to a student's portfolio, is a stakeholder. There may be several secondary stakeholders—teachers, peers, parents, administrators, those who collect school assessment data, district officials, learning specialists. Every audience has differing reasons or needs in relationship to the portfolios. Each will probably look for different things when they view a Writing Portfolio.

TEACHERS play an important role in portfolio development. Students need a teacher to be their guide and partner as they learn the process of using portfolios. Of course, the teacher has a vested interest in the portfolio for purposes such as knowledge of the student, instructional improvement and assessment.

In most classrooms, it is desirable for teachers to retain some say in decisions about the portfolios. The level of teacher control or guidance will depend on the age and ability of the students as well as on the portfolio purposes.

For many teachers, there is a strong temptation to keep primary control over the development, contents and processes of the portfolios. This is a temptation to be heartily resisted! Benefits such as student independence, sense of self as a writer, responsibility for learning and ability to self-assess increase as the student's sense of portfolio ownership increases. Excessive control by the teacher will very likely lessen the degree to which the portfolio reflects the student's true writing capabilities and growth.

Attention Teachers!
RESIST THE URGE TO TAKE OVER THE PORTFOLIOS

PARENTS almost always have an interest in their children's portfolios. This is an audience to be seriously considered. Numerous benefits will result when parents are kept informed and involved in the portfolio process. They can learn and contribute a great deal when they are invited to participate in some way.

PEERS have a natural interest in one another's portfolios. Most students are eager to share some or all of their portfolio contents with their classmates and friends. Access to other portfolios provides stimulation for writing, appreciation for others' work, and a great basis for good writing instruction. Students also learn new skills as they respond to and reflect on writing of peers.

ADMINISTRATORS and other school officials are often interested in having access to student portfolios. This may be to assist a student's learning, gather assessment data, improve the curriculum, learn about how young writers are developing, or communicate with the community. Many districts have an interest in passing student portfolios along from year to year for documenting ongoing growth and achievement.

Portfolios give parents and administrators insights they could never get from test scores or report cards.

PARENT'S NIGHT WELCOME !

Lisa's Portfolio 3rd Grade

TEACHING THE WRITING PROCESS

The use of Writing Portfolios in the classroom is based on some assumptions about the writing instruction currently taking place:

1) students have been acquainted with the writing process

2) students are having experiences using the writing process

3) students are doing lots of writing

4) students are writing in a variety of styles and modes for a variety of purposes and a variety of audiences

5) students are writing on topics that are meaningful and relevant to them

6) students have some choice in their writing topics

Writing Portfolios only work where students are using the writing process.

WRITE OFTEN...WITH VARIETY

In order for students to have a rich collection of writing for portfolios, it is necessary for them to have a variety of writing experiences. As a part of your writing instruction, design activities that inspire students to read and write all kinds of things—short and long. Get them writing several times each week. This will give them a chance to fill their Working Portfolios with plenty of raw and finished material for motivating writing, reflecting, revising, re-visiting and comparing. Pages 36–37 will give you examples of some of the kinds of writing kids can do.

A MODEL FOR LEARNING THE PROCESS

Students can write volumes on their own and never improve their writing processes. The writing process must be taught to them. It is my bias that the writing process is best learned under the skilled direction of a human being—a teacher guiding and modeling the process with and for the students. For teachers beginning or expanding teaching of writing as a process, these steps offer a way to proceed:

Teachers who love writing do wonders for kids

1) Be thoroughly acquainted with the writing process yourself. Practice it in your own writing. (See **Teacher's Review**, pages 30–31.)

2) Do several pieces of writing together as a group, guiding the students through the process of creating and polishing a collaborative piece.

3) Let students work on pieces of writing in pairs or small groups, again with clear direction through the steps of the process.

4) Spend time talking about the different steps of the process. Stop sometimes and concentrate on just one step.

5) Gradually move to individual writing within a group setting where you can orchestrate the moves through the process steps.

6) When students have enough experience with the process so that they can handle it on their own, they can work independently, with a written guide to the writing process steps handy. (See **The Kid's Guide to the Writing Process**, page 35.)

TEACHING THE WRITING PROCESS continued...

TEACHER'S REVIEW OF THE WRITING PROCESS

STEP 1   ROMANCING

This is the reason for writing...the motivator...the spark that gets ideas brewing. A thought, a piece of literature, a discussion, an activity, a feeling, an opinion—something has happened that gets students excited about writing or begins to dislodge thoughts and words. This may start with an activity you design, or you may help students grab on to something that's already there inside them. Spend plenty of time on this stage. When kids don't want to write or can't think of anything to say, usually it's because they haven't been romanced enough.

STEP 2   COLLECTING

This is the most fun and creative part of the process. It is the stage where writers brainstorm; jot down words, ideas, phrases and thoughts; gather bits and pieces. Allow time for lots of collecting. Write down everything. Writers can always eliminate, expand, combine later.

STEP 3   ORGANIZING

In this step, writers take a look at what has been collected, think about what fits with what, and begin to pull ideas together in some way. This might be done with lines, diagrams, clusters, outlines, webs or lists.

STEP 4   DRAFTING

Here's where the writing actually begins. Writers look at the groupings and start to put ideas together into lines, sentences or paragraphs.

STEP 5   REVIEWING

The writer gives the piece a quick overview before going on to solicit responses to the writing—just to see if the draft generally says and does what the writer intended.

STEP 6   SHARING FOR PRAISES AND QUESTIONS

The writer asks someone else to review and respond to the writing. That response can be in the form of praise or compliments and questions or suggestions. For example:

This phrase icy fingers of fog really gave me a chill. It made me feel what it's like to be out in cold fog.

The opening word Crash! really grabbed my interest.

You chose wonderful wet words for your rain poem—slush, slurp, drizzle, sloshing, soggy.

Did you mean to give the ending away so soon?

STEP 7   REVISING

Making use of the response gained from other readers, the writer revises, replaces, adds, deletes, rearranges or otherwise strengthens and changes the piece.

STEP 8   CHECKING MECHANICS

This is the place for checking and correcting spelling and mechanics. Students may need a peer, teacher, editing committee or adult helper to do this.

STEP 9   FINAL POLISHING

At this point the writer has decided that the piece is finished and fixed enough for a final, accurate copy. This copy may be written, dictated to a transcriber, typed on a computer, recorded on tape or otherwise completed.

STEP 10   SHOWING OFF

The writer should always have the option of sharing, publishing or otherwise showcasing the writing. There are unlimited ways to do this. Students can be encouraged to find appropriate and inviting ways to share writing.

TIPS FOR TEACHING THE WRITING PROCESS

1) **Saturate them with literature.** Writing flourishes in a classroom that's loaded with literature—lots of it—of many kinds. Literature serves as a motivator. It sparks ideas. It lets kids see that there are so many ways to say something and so many things to write about. Bring as much "written stuff" into your classroom as possible, and read, read, read.

2) **Sensitize them to everyday experiences.** Let your students know that they can write about **anything**. The subject can be something that is earth-shattering or seemingly inconsequential; sad or funny or happy; silly or serious; private or public. Help them see that there are words for telling about virtually everything.

3) **Provide meaningful writing activities.** Only ask students to write about topics that are of relevance to them and their lives. They'll have more to say and they'll write better.

4) **Give them plenty of choice.** All writers do better writing when the topic is interesting and personally appealing. Allow them as much choice as possible, even when you're working with one genre or theme. Writers are always much more willing and eager to write when they own the topic.

5) **You write, too.** When you write at the same time your students are writing, it changes everything. Model use of the process for your students, share your writing with them at all stages and let them help you.

6) **Try plenty of short forms.** It is far easier for a student to handle the whole writing process when working with short pieces of writing. Those long stories that go on forever and ever are very difficult to revise and polish. Be alert to the many shorter kinds of writing that can be used well to teach the writing process.

7) **Don't always go through the whole process.** If students have to do a complete workover on every single piece of writing, they'll quit writing—or grow to hate it. Every stage of the process is important. Students have had a real and valuable writing experience even if they put a piece aside after a few stages.

8) **Emphasize the process.** Dwell on various stages. Bring in an author to show works at various stages. Talk a lot about each step, ask questions, discuss what makes each step important. Remember that the process is more important than the product.

9) **Write together—often.** When you introduce a new form, when writers seem stuck, when a topic is difficult or when a topic has grabbed everybody—go back to writing as a class. Besides being fun and satisfying, collaborative writing refreshes and reinforces the process.

10) **Allow plenty of time.** Give students the time they really need to work through the whole writing process. Good writing cannot and should not be rushed.

HOW PORTFOLIOS FIT IN

The portfolio concept seems ready-made for a partnership with the writing process. Portfolios have the potential to support many facets of good writing instruction. Here's how:

- Portfolios allow students to gather and save a variety of kinds of writing on many topics. This collection is available for students to work on various stages of the writing process.

- Portfolios can be a place where a writer showcases pieces of writing at various stages of the process.

- Portfolios can showcase one work throughout all the process stages.

- Portfolios can reveal to students and teachers the successes and struggles they are having with the writing process.

- Portfolios provide a way for the writers to see **how** they use the process.

- Portfolios can show the teacher how the students are learning and thinking about the writing process.

The Writing Portfolio is a rich resource for writing instruction. However, just because there are Writing Portfolios in a classroom does not insure that good writing is going on. Portfolios only lead to effective writing instruction if they are successfully designed and used for that purpose. As you continue with this book, you will find guidelines for portfolio use that will help your portfolio process lead to good writing instruction. (In particular, see **Portfolios and Writing Instruction,** pages 106–110.)

The Kid's Guide To The Writing Process

STEP 1   ROMANCING
This is the starter—something that gets ideas flowing. It can be something you see, hear, remember, feel or something you have experienced—anything that interests you and gets you thinking.

STEP 2   COLLECTING
Write down <u>everything</u> you can think of that has to do with the topic...words or phrases or ideas or sentences or thoughts.

STEP 3   ORGANIZING
Take the ideas and start seeing which ones go together. Use a diagram or lines or boxes or clusters or a web.

STEP 4   DRAFTING
Start writing. Use your groups of ideas to create lines or sentences to say what you think you want to say.

STEP 5   REVIEWING
Do a quick read-through of what you've written to make sure no words or ideas are left out, no sentences are unfinished and to see if it says what you intended it to say.

STEP 6   SHARING FOR PRAISES AND QUESTIONS
Ask someone else to read your writing and tell you what's good about it, point out what they like about it, ask questions and give ideas for changes or improvements.

STEP 7   REVISING
Use your own ideas and responses from others to change, add, rearrange, remove, write more or otherwise revise anything you think needs to be improved or changed.

STEP 8   CHECKING MECHANICS
Correct spelling, grammar and punctuation.

STEP 9   FINAL POLISHING
Recopy carefully (or type) a clean, accurate copy after you've decided on changes and corrections.

STEP 10   SHOWING OFF
If you wish, find a way to share, publish or show off what you've written.

write on

TRY WRITING THESE...

advertisements
advice columns
anecdotes
announcements
apologies
arguments
autobiographies
awards

ballads
bedtime stories
beginnings
billboards
biographies
book jackets
book reviews
bulletins
bumper stickers

campaign speeches
cartoons
captions
catalog entries
cereal boxes
certificates
character sketches
cinquains
codes
comic strips
comparisons
complaints
contracts
conversations
critiques

definitions
descriptions
dialogues
diamantes
diaries
diets
directions
directories
dramas
dreams

editorials
epilogues
epitaphs
endings
essays
exaggerations
exclamations
explanations

fables
fairy tales
fantasies
folklore
fortunes
funny tales

game rules
**good news -
  bad news**
greeting cards
grocery lists
gossip

impromptu speeches
inquiries
interview questions
introductions
invitations

jingles
job applications
jokes
journals

legends
letters
lists
love notes
lyrics

magazine articles
memories
metaphors
menus
monologues
movie reviews
movie scripts
mysteries
myths

newscasts
newspapers
notebooks
nursery rhymes

observations
odes
opinions

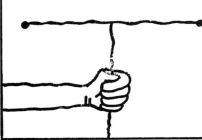

pamphlets
parables
paragraphs
parodies
persuasions
phrases
plays
poems
post cards
post scripts
posters
predictions
problems
problem solutions
prologues
proposals
propaganda
protests
proverbs
puppet shows
puns
puzzles

quips
quizzes
questions
quotations

real estate notices
rebuttals
recipes
record covers
remedies
reports
requests
resumés
reviews
riddles
rhymes

sales pitches
satires
schedules
secrets
self descriptions
sentences
sequels
signs
silly sayings
skywriting messages
slogans
songs
song titles
speeches
spoofs
spooky stories
spoonerisms
sports analyses
sports reports
supestitions

TV commercials
TV guides
TV programs
tall tales
telegrams
telephone messages
thank-you notes
theater programs
titles
tongue twisters
traffic rules
travel brochures
travel posters
tributes
trivia

vignettes
vitas

want ads
wanted posters
warnings
wills
wise sayings
wishes
weather reports
weather forecasts
wonderful words

yarns
yellow pages

WRITE TO..

persuade
delight
convince
explain
surprise
amuse
trigger
   imagination
expound
disturb
question
entertain

KINDS OF WRITING PORTFOLIOS

Writing Portfolios come in all kinds, shapes and sizes. They may be simple or complex. They may be relatively unstructured or highly structured. They may have few or many writing samples.

NO "RIGHT" KIND OF PORTFOLIO

No one can tell you exactly what kind of Writing Portfolio your students should create, because there is no one right or best kind. Each portfolio project should be designed locally or individually by teachers and students using them. However, it is crucial that **the kind of portfolio be determined by the purposes and uses of the portfolio, based on the needs of the student and classroom.**

Most Writing Portfolios generally fall into these categories:

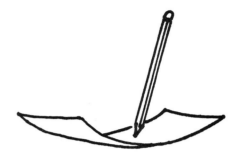

The kind of portfolio is determined by its purposes.

THE WORKING PORTFOLIO

A dual portfolio filing system is highly desirable for students. First, each student has a Working Portfolio or storage folder. It is for keeping a substantial number of elements of the student's writing and writing–related work. This is the source from which pieces are selected to move into the Writing Portfolio or Showcase Portfolio.

Students and teachers together should decide which things to put into the Working Portfolio. It is important to keep a wide variety of selections from school and from home. These should represent many kinds of writing for many purposes over a period of time. Keep work that shows each part of the writing process, works in progress and finished works. (See pages 47–51.)

SHOWCASE PORTFOLIO

This may be referred to as **The Writing Portfolio** or **The Portfolio** or **The Showcase Portfolio**. Whatever name it's given, it is a collection of writing selected to showcase for particular purposes. It is the Writing Portfolio as defined on page 14.

Work is selected for a particular reason and/or according to specific criteria from the rich collection in the Working Portfolio. The work is moved into the Showcase Portfolio.

Individual portfolio contents will vary according to the purposes of the portfolio and the particular portfolio system.

Selections are made at times agreed upon within the classroom. This may happen once a month, at the end of a grading period, twice a year, or on an ongoing basis. It all depends on the system that has been chosen.

This Showcase Portfolio includes more than a collection of pieces of writing. Student self-reflections and evaluations are of major importance to the Showcase Portfolio. Other elements, such as writing attitude or interest inventories, conference notes, parent or peer reflections, and illustrations may be included as well. (See pages 52–58 for sample contents.)

The key concept to understand about the Showcase Portfolio is that items in it have been carefully selected and moved into it for a purpose.

Each item in the Showcase Writing Portfolio is there for a particular reason.

Many schools or districts want students to build portfolios over several years.

THE PASS-ALONG PORTFOLIO

In some cases, students might need or want a portfolio at the end of the year that is a bit different from the ongoing Writing Portfolio.

Here's how it may differ. The Showcase Portfolio that is built during the year for instructional or assessment purposes (or both) probably includes selections that students want to be seen only within that classroom. But the school or district may wish to have student portfolios for other purposes, such as to pass on to the next teacher or have reviewed for collecting district data. Specific requirements or limits may be set for the portfolios that are used for district purposes.

In that case, students may want to create a Final, Pass-Along or Year-End Portfolio. This might involve adding, deleting or replacing entries from the Showcase Portfolio. This Final Portfolio will include copies of selections the student feels comfortable putting forth for public scrutiny.

THE COMPUTER PORTFOLIO

Portfolios don't have to be stored in folders or boxes. Some students or classes wish to keep Writing Portfolios on computer. This is very workable in some settings. Many elements in any Writing Portfolios, including graphics and illustrations, can be created and stored on computer.

If a computer is the main source for creating and storing Writing Portfolios, make sure that students create a **User's Guide** so peers, teachers and others can easily access and review portfolios when necessary. And at times writers will need to print out hard copies of all or some portfolio entries for reading and response by others.

TEACHER'S PERSONAL PORTFOLIO

It is heartily recommended that the teacher keep a Writing Portfolio of the same nature as the one kept by students. The teacher should follow any guidelines and structures that have been set for the student Writing Portfolios. This is an excellent way for the teacher to model good learning behaviors. It's also a good way for the teacher to see and show herself or himself as a writer. The portfolio process helps teachers grow as writers, just as it helps students grow.

CLASS PROFILE—WRITING PORTFOLIO CRITERIA

Teacher **Steven James**   School Year **93-94**

Student	Variety and Quantity of Writing	Use of Writing Techniques	Use of Writing Process	Mechanics	Evidence of Writing Growth	Facility with Portfolio Processes	Personal Involvement and Attitude
Amy C	ok	ok	+	ok	ok	ok	+
Brad N	++	-	ok	ok	ok	ok	+
Chad R	ok	-	ok	-	ok	ok	++
Chen Y	ok	ok	-	ok	ok	ok	+
Jonathan L	- variety ok quantity	-	ok	-	ok	ok	+
Juanita T	ok	-	ok	ok	+	ok	+
Kate B.	- born	ok	ok	ok	+	ok	+
Maria V.	++	ok	ok	+	ok	ok	+
Meadow L.	++	+	-	+	ok	ok	+
Nate F.	ok	-	-	ok	+	ok	+
Sam K.	ok	ok	ok	+	+	ok	+
Samantha	- variety ok quantity	ok	+	+	ok	ok	+
William	++	ok	+	-	+	ok	+
Adam V.	ok	-	-	ok	+	ok	+

+ doing this very well   — needs help or improve
ok acceptable

TEACHER'S ASSESSMENT PORTFOLIO

Many teachers have found this to be a workable way to keep records on student portfolios. Some keep an Assessment Portfolio on each student. Others design one Classroom Assessment Portfolio that holds information on all students.

The Assessment Portfolio will contain any information that the teacher wishes to gather to assist in assessment and to keep records of student self-assessment. Possible items are:

- evaluation or criteria checklists
- guidelines for analytic scoring of writing
- scores from analytic scoring of student writing
- copies of Contents Table from student Portfolios
- copies of selections from student portfolios
- notes from conferences with students
- charts for keeping records of student portfolio progress or portfolio conferences
- or any other data the teacher needs to keep for purposes of tracking, helping or assessing student portfolio use and progress.

©1994 by Incentive Publications, Inc., Nashville, TN.

WHAT DOES A WRITING PORTFOLIO LOOK LIKE?

A Writing Portfolio can have many looks. There is
no one kind of container or appearance that is
right for all portfolios. The size and shape of the
portfolio should be determined by:

- the purposes and goals of the portfolio

- the type of portfolio

- the needs of the students

- the needs of the classroom

THE IMPORTANCE OF THE CONTAINER

It may seem that the real meat of the Writing
Portfolio is the collection of writing samples and
reflections that are contained inside. However, the
outside, the design, the inside covers, the inside
organization, the personal touches added—are also
integral parts of the portfolio process. The sense of
student ownership and commitment to the portfolio begin with the choosing and designing of the
container—inside and out.

Decisions about the looks of the Writing Portfolios
can be made through teacher-student discussion.
In some classrooms, students choose different
kinds of containers, according to individual needs
and tastes. When considering containers, think
about the convenience of storing portfolios that are
not uniform in size and shape.

CONTAINER CHOICES

There are dozens of options for the outside container of a Writing Portfolio. These are some examples already in use in classrooms:

- student-made construction paper folders
- commercial file folders of various sizes
- accordion file folders
- commercial cardboard architect-type folders
- student-made architect folders
- small cardboard boxes
- large mailing envelopes
- folders designed for hanging files
- wire baskets
- stackable bins or plastic dishpans

RULES FOR CHOOSING THE CONTAINER

1) Think about your space. The container must not cause space or management problems.

2) The portfolio must be big and sturdy enough to hold all the elements students will put in it.

3) It must be small enough for the student to carry around.

4) It must be convenient for students and the teacher to get to and use.

5) Students should have a part in choosing and creating their own containers.

How the portfolio looks is an important part of the process.

DESIGNING THE CONTAINER

The first step the writer takes towards ownership of the portfolio is to design the container. As the writer puts those beginning efforts into conceiving the design, he or she is already allowing the portfolio to say: "This is who I am as a thinker and writer and person."

Allow plenty of time and materials for students to design portfolios that reflect themselves. Let them think about the ideas and work on the designs over a period of several days. Provide lots of supplies such as brightly colored papers, crayons, markers, paints, stickers. Encourage them to include art work, computer graphics, pictures cut from magazines, photographs, etc.

Not only does this part of the process begin to tell the stories of individual writers, it is great fun! The excitement about portfolios really starts here.

As the teacher, you'll start learning new things about your students as you watch them design their Writing Portfolios.

And, by the way—don't forget to create and design your own portfolio at the same time. Make sure it tells who you are.

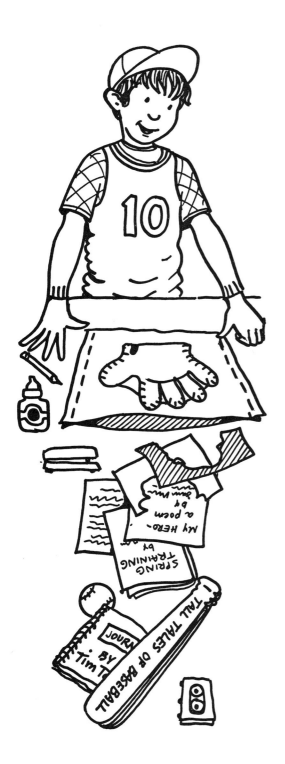

WAYS TO PERSONALIZE PORTFOLIOS

As you and your students are creating personal Writing Portfolios, encourage use of techniques and elements that reflect students' individual ideas, interests and personalities, such as:

- outside design showing a particular interest (for instance: computer graphics for a computer buff, pictures of gymnastics for a gymnast, etc.)

- designs made with your name or initials

- a favorite theme or color scheme chosen to repeat throughout the design

- photographs of self, home, family, friends, pets, interests on outside or inside cover

- "ME" artwork—such as handprints or head silhouette filled with words about you

- an audio or video cassette tape introducing yourself and your portfolio to any readers

- personal treasures from outside school

- an autobiographical sketch on the back cover

- a frame showing off favorite words

- a photo essay about an interest of yours

- a "Don't Look at This Portfolio Until You Read This..." Letter

- a list of favorite pieces of literature

- an "About Myself" list with favorite (and unfavorite) things, activities, etc.

WHAT'S IN A WRITING PORTFOLIO?

The contents of the Writing Portfolio vary as widely as the containers. There is no set of contents that is best for all classrooms. As is true with choices of containers, the decisions about what goes inside any Writing Portfolio must be based on the purposes of the portfolio.

Unlimited possibilities for portfolio elements exist, even with a portfolio that focuses primarily on one curriculum area. The following pages will suggest possible elements, recommend some essentials, and give you several sample contents pages for differing Writing Portfolios.

IT STARTS WITH THE WORKING PORTFOLIO

Even before the main Writing Portfolio or Showcase Portfolio is designed, the collecting should begin. That's what the Working Portfolio is all about. It is the source for any selections that will be moved into the Writing Portfolio. Thus, it needs to be kept well supplied with the raw material for use in the portfolio process.

It is neither necessary nor desirable to keep every piece of writing or writing-related work in the Working Portfolio. Students and teacher can decide together what to keep. Or the student and the teacher may each make additions to the Working Portfolio. Parents and peers might also suggest that an item be kept in the Working Portfolio.

Collect lots of writing samples and other writing-related "stuff"—from inside and outside school.

WHAT TO COLLECT

It is important that the Working Portfolio have enough of the kinds of elements that will suit the purposes of the classroom portfolio process. Here are some guidelines that may help:

1) Collect a variety of kinds of writing.

2) Collect writing done for different purposes and audiences.

3) Collect writing done in and out of school.

4) Keep writing samples throughout the year.

5) Collect samples that represent different stages in the writing process.

6) Keep witing that is in process as well as finished writing.

7) Keep treasures, favorite items, pictures, pieces of literature, word lists, ideas and other things that may serve as starters for writing.

8) Save some pieces of writing from other curriculum areas.

9) Collect work or samples that relate to writing, such as: Writing Attitude Inventories, Lists of Favorite Books, etc.

10) Save notes, comments and suggestions on writing from peers, teacher, others.

11) Keep tools that serve as writing helpers—such as writing skills lists, editing guide, explanation of writing traits and modes.

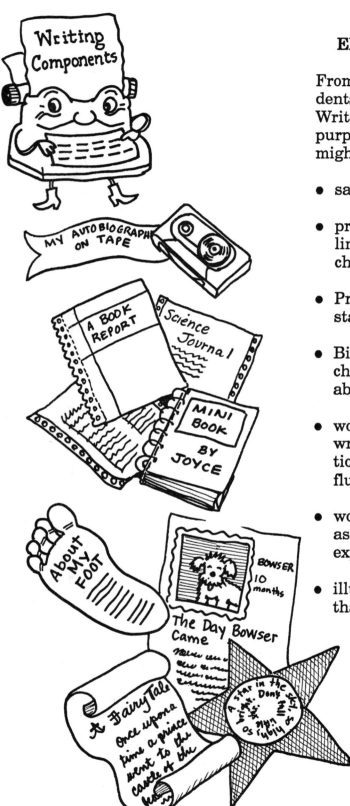

ELEMENTS IN THE WRITING PORTFOLIO

From the collection in the Working Portfolio, students will be selecting samples to move into the Writing Portfolio that showcases work for some purpose. These are some of the kinds of work that might be moved into the Showcase Portfolio:

- samples of different kinds of writing

- pre-writing examples—for example: webs, outlines, clusters, collections of phrases, words, charts, ideas, etc.

- Process Package—a work shown through all stages of the writing process

- Biography of a Work—a written explanation, chart or diagram, detailing how the writer went about creating the work

- works that show evidence of the various writing traits—such as word choice, organization, ideas and content, clarity, voice, sentence fluency, conventions

- work that reflects various modes of writing such as descriptive, imaginative, persuasive, expository, narrative

- illustrations, graphics or photos that were created to accompany writing

- writing within artwork (i.e., cartoons, posters, storyboards, advertisements)

- items, notes, ideas or other examples of something that sparked writing

- works in progress
- finished works
- pieces that show responses to literature
- journal entries
- home writing projects
- writing interest inventory
- writing attitude inventory
- photo essay
- display of special or favorite words
- mini-books
- piece written for a specific audience
- audiotape of an original written work
- videotape which student created
- writing from other subject areas
- early piece/later piece
- pieces from various times of the year
- favorite piece
- important piece
- satisfying piece
- unsatisfying piece
- best piece
- piece that gave me trouble
- most exciting piece
- fun piece
- piece I'd like to do over
- piece that tells about me
- piece I'd like to throw away
- free pick
- teacher pick
- parent pick
- a piece scored on a scoring rubric
- student comparisons of pieces
- student self-reflections on pieces
- comments or reflection from a peer
- comments or reflection from parent
- comments or reflection from the teacher
- self-reflections on the whole portfolio
- letter to teacher before the conference

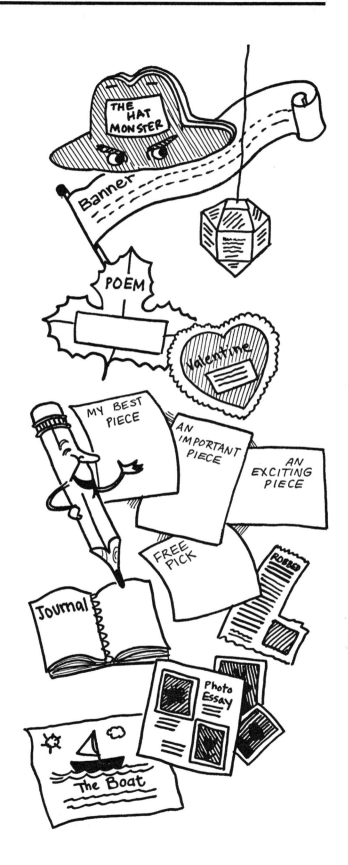

ABSOLUTE ESSENTIALS

No matter what the age, ability, or writing experience of the student, it seems that there are some elements necessary for inclusion if the portfolio is to truly meet the definition outlined for a Writing Portfolio. Here are the essentials:

- A Contents List or other Cover Sheet detailing what is in the portfolio

- Multiple samples

- A variety of kinds of writing

- Samples collected over time

- Dates on all entries

- Samples that show evidence of growth

- A letter or statement of introduction or some other place where the type and purpose of the portfolio are explained by the author

- Criteria or reasons for each selection

- Evidence that student took part in selection

- Student self-reflection on all or some of the pieces of writing

And if the portfolio is to be used for assessment purposes:

- Some evidence of the criteria used for evaluating pieces of writing and/or for judging the whole portfolio

What does "Absolute Essentials for the Writing Portfolio" mean?

It means you'd better have it in there!

HIGHLY RECOMMENDED COMPONENTS

In addition to the "musts" for Writing Portfolios, some other components are highly recommended. If they are appropriate to your students' capabilities and the portfolio's purposes, do consider including these:

● a "package" showing a piece of writing through all steps in the writing process

● a "biography" of one piece of writing— explaining how the writing was done

● at least one piece of writing from another subject area

● some writing done outside of school and without an assignment from school

● one or more pieces that represent a free pick by the student—something chosen by the student for any stated reason

● at least one piece that reflects some struggle or difficulty the student has in writing

● a comparison of an early piece with a later piece

● a reflection by another person

● some sort of reflection on the portfolio as a whole

THE CONTENTS PAGE

At the very front of every Writing Portfolio, any reader should be able to find a cover sheet that supplies the following information:

Student name

Teacher or class

Dates covered by portfolio

Title or type of portfolio

Purpose of portfolio

List of Components (and why each was chosen)

A Letter Written by the Student to the Audience
    This might include the purposes of the portfolio,
    an explanation of what the portfolio shows
    about the writer, and anything else the author
    of the portfolio wishes to tell the audience.

"Here is a sample Contents Page..."

Jerome's Writing Portfolio

Letter to All Readers

"Oh, No!"--My Best Work from the Fall

"Why Do Grownups Always Hurry?"--My Best Work from the Spring

"What Friends are For"--My Most Serious Writing

"Can Sisters Be Trusted?"--My Favorite Work

Self-Reflections on all pieces

Parent Reflection on "What Friends Are For"

Conference Notes

Sara's Writing Portfolio

by <u>Sara MacPherson</u>   Grade   <u>4</u>

Teacher: <u>Mr. Bridges</u>   Lincoln School

Contents

1. My letter to the audience explaining my portfolio's purpose and telling what I want readers to know about my portfolio.

2. "<u>The Disaster</u>" - my favorite piece

3. My reflection on "<u>The Disaster</u>"

4. "<u>You Never Know About Green</u>" -a poem- Process Package

5. My reflection on "You Never Know About Green" and the process

6. "<u>Ode To My Hockey Stick</u>" -an early piece

7. "<u>The Worst Vacation Ever</u>" - a later piece

8. My comparison of the early and later pieces

9. "<u>It's Good To Have A Brother</u>" - an important piece

10. My reflection on my important piece

11. My metacognitive letter about my portfolio

PORTFOLIO STRUCTURE

Writing Portfolios do—and should—vary widely in the kind and amount of structure. They may have very little structure or be very highly structured or fall anywhere in between. There are no exact rules to follow when you and your students settle on the kind of structure. This depends on the portfolio purposes and the needs of the students. However, do keep in mind:

1) Student choice is fundamental to the process, so don't neglect including plenty of student-selected elements.

2) Student ownership and motivation are seriously affected when the teacher, administrators or others have too much control over the portfolio.

3) Left with no structure, students may be unable to make selections which demonstrate variety, versatility and growth.

4) Students will grow and change in their ability to make decisions and handle their portfolios proficiently.

5) Decisions about structure should take place through discussion with teachers and students working as partners.

6) Whatever the structure of the portfolio, it is crucial that students understand how it works and what the reasons are behind it.

7) Most classes end up designing and using portfolios that fall somewhere in the middle between unstructured and highly structured.

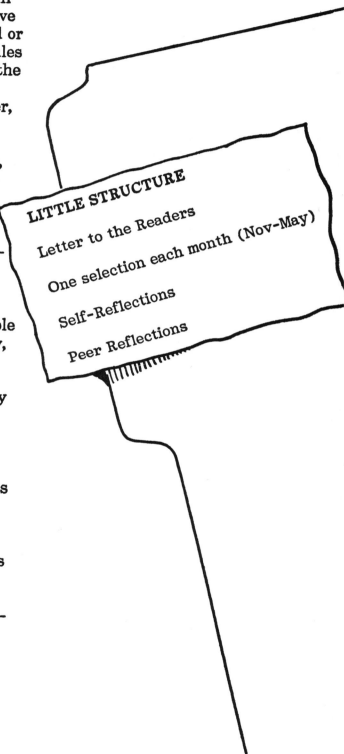

LITTLE STRUCTURE

Letter to the Readers

One selection each month (Nov-May)

Self-Reflections

Peer Reflections

HIGHLY STRUCTURED

A Letter to the Audience

One piece from each category: descriptive, narrative, expository, imaginative, persuasive

A business letter

An outline used to write one work

A comparison of two book reports--Where the Red Fern Grows and Tom Sawyer

Reflections on each piece

Portfolio evaluation

HIGHLY STRUCTURED

Letter about Portfolio

Written response to There's a Monster in my Closet

Thanksgiving poem

Thank you letter for holiday gifts

A piece written about winter

5 questions about the Space Unit

3 Self-Reflections

1 Parent Reflection

MODERATE STRUCTURE

Letter about the portfolio
A work shown through the writing process
A work from another subject area
3 free picks
A piece of writing done at home
An unfinished work
Self-reflections
Peer and parent reflections

MODERATE STRUCTURE

Introduction to the Portfolio
An important piece
A piece I'm really proud of
A piece I'd like to throw away
A piece that shows how I handled one particular stage of the writing process
A free pick
A teacher pick
Self-reflections

LITTLE STRUCTURE

Introductory Letter

4-6 samples chosen for any reason (Must be different kinds of writing and show writing over several months.)

Self-reflections on selections

My Writing Portfolio

- a project from home
- a photo essay
- a video tape I wrote and created
- my most surprising work
- two journal entries
- illustrated work
- a free pick
- self-reflections
- teacher, peer, and parent reflections

Writing Portfolio Contents

Letter from the Author
An idea web
A first draft
A finished piece
A piece I feel good about
A piece I'd like to
  throw away
My best work
Self-Reflections
End-of-Year Letter

MY WRITING PORTFOLIO

Please read this letter

Show-Off poster of favorite words

Fall sample and reflection

Winter sample and reflection

Spring sample and reflection

My most important writing

Final letter

WRITING PORTFOLIO CONTENTS

LETTER TO READERS

BEST PIECE

FUNNIEST PIECE

IMPORTANT PIECE

EARLY PIECE AND LATER PIECE

REFLECTIONS ON PIECES

LETTER TO TEACHER ABOUT
"HOW I'VE CHANGED AS A WRITER"

WRITING PORTFOLIO CONTENTS

LETTER OF PURPOSE
PRE-WRITING SAMPLES
A WORK THROUGH THE WRITING PROCESS
A WRITING INTEREST INVENTORY
A JOURNAL ENTRY
A REPORT FROM ANOTHER SUBJECT
AN EXPOSITORY ESSAY
A PERSUASIVE WORK
3 FREE PICKS OF DIFFERENT KINDS
OF WRITING
A WORK I STRUGGLED WITH
SELF-REFLECTIONS
CONFERENCE CHECKLISTS
FINAL METACOGNITIVE LETTER
EVALUATING PORTFOLIO PROCESS

WRITING PORTFOLIO CONTENTS

PORTFOLIO LETTER
MY BEST WORK
AN UNFINISHED WORK
AN EARLY WORK
A LATER WORK
TWO OTHER WORKS — FREE PICK
A BIOGRAPHY OF ONE WORK
AN ILLUSTRATED WORK
SELF-EVALUATIONS
PEER EDITING GROUP COMMENTS
PARENT COMMENTS
FINAL LETTER

Writing Portfolio Contents

1. Letter about me and my portfolio.
2. Three favorite pieces.
3. A piece the teacher picks.
4. Four journal entries.
5. A book report.
6. A tape of me reading something I wrote.
7. Self-reflections

WRITING PORTFOLIO

LETTER ABOUT THE PORTFOLIO AND THE WRITER

A WORK IN PROCESS

5 SAMPLES OF DIFFERENT KINDS OF WRITING

A BEST PIECE

CRITERIA CHECKLISTS

SELF-REFLECTIONS

TEACHER COMMENTS

PARENT COMMENTS

FINAL REFLECTION ON WHOLE PORTFOLIO

Writing Portfolio Contents

A letter "about my portfolio"

My best writing

My favorite writing

A November Sample

A May Sample

Pictures and drawings

My

Writing Portfolio

Introductory Letter

Writing Attitude Inventory - Beginning of Year

A mini book

A poem

A story

A description

A fall piece and a spring piece - and a comparison

A free pick

A teacher pick

Something written at home

Self-reflections

Writing Attitudes Inventory - End of Year

Final reflections on portfolio

WRITING PORTFOLIO CONTENTS

LETTER TO THE AUDIENCE

PIECES OF PRE-WRITING

WRITING INTEREST INVENTORY

A WORK IN PROGRESS

A PHOTO ESSAY

A MOST FAVORITE PIECE

A TROUBLING PIECE

A MOST IMPORTANT PIECE

A PIECE FROM SCIENCE OR SOCIAL STUDIES

A BEST PIECE

LETTERS TO TEACHERS BEFORE CONFERENCES

SELF-REFLECTIONS

PEER EDITOR COMMENTS

FINAL REFLECTION ON THE PORTFOLIO

II. DEVELOPING AND USING
WRITING PORTFOLIOS

BEFORE YOU BEGIN USING WRITING PORTFOLIOS

Most teachers involved in portfolio projects insist that the key to success is **planning**. The better prepared you are when you start the process—for portfolios of any kind—the more likely you are to end up accomplishing the goals you set.

So before you actually begin development of your writing portfolios, take time to do the necessary thinking and planning. Here are some of the pre-portfolio considerations that you may focus on.

BASIC ASSUMPTIONS

Beneath the Writing Portfolio process are some underlying assumptions and values:

- that the process of writing and the teaching of writing are important and worth appropriate amounts of classroom time

- that teachers and students can learn more about writing from watching students do the process than from reading finished products

- that students are able to make decisions about their own learning

- that students can and should be seriously involved in evaluation of their writing

- that writing assessment is intricately tied to writing instruction

- that students have valid ideas about procedures and can participate meaningfully in the design of a portfolio system

I'd like to write about my new little kitty.

The portfolio classroom is student-centered, not teacher-centered.

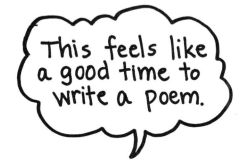

This feels like a good time to write a poem.

THE RIGHT CLIMATE FOR PORTFOLIOS

There is a particular "feel" or climate in a classroom where Writing Portfolios are being used with success. Observation in such a classroom shows that it is a place where:

- student input is solicited and valued

- students believe that the teacher sees them as equal partners in learning

- students feel trusted and respected

- the teacher is able to share power and responsibility for learning with the students

- teachers create writing assignments that encourage students to make their own choices, to take risks, to be original, and to make new discoveries

- students feel they have enough time to think, write, discuss, revise, make decisions

- writing takes place in a workshop atmosphere where the learners and teacher are actively involved and free to interact with each other

- the teacher really listens to students and adapts instruction and procedures to meet their needs

Students need to know that they are equal partners in their learning.

I want to write my story about the rainforest using cartoon characters.

CHANGES IN ROLES

As you have already seen, the portfolio process involves a departure from traditional classroom proceedings. The roles of the teacher and the students are quite different from what has been the norm in many classrooms. If you are beginning to use portfolios as a part of your writing or language arts instruction, you may find yourself faced with some necessary changes.

In a classroom where portfolios are used, the teacher is not the main decision maker, holding the total responsibility for designing and orchestrating learning situations. Instead, the teacher serves as a guide, working in a close partnership with students. This involves a "letting go" on the part of the teacher. For students, the major changes are learning to make choices, taking more responsibility for learning and leaning less on the teacher for decision making.

Changes in roles do not happen overnight. But the teacher must be willing to work for the necessary changes, let them happen, and nurture students to be equal partners. If a teacher is committed to these goals, students and teacher can learn and grow together gradually as they gain practice with the portfolio process.

Portfolio use will require re-thinking classroom roles.

Instead of being decision-maker, the teacher helps students become decision-makers.

Let's invite our families to a party to show off our portfolios.

DECISIONS TO BE MADE

Several decisions need to be made before you start making and using Writing Portfolios in the classroom. Think these through carefully before the portfolio concept is introduced to the students. **But don't leave students out of the decisions.** Most of these can and should be discussed with students before final plans are made. Once you've introduced the concept to students, there will be plenty of chances to discuss decisions, such as those that follow, with them.

Although you'll want to consider these kinds of questions now, be aware that some of the answers will not take shape entirely until you are underway with portfolios. This is particularly true with questions about the management system. You and your students will learn, come up with better ideas, discover different possibilities and make changes as you go along.

DON'T BEGIN UNTIL YOU...

Do A Climate Check

- Do the classroom conditions exist which will allow the portfolio process to succeed?

- Is the teacher ready for the changes in roles that will take place?

Establish Ownership

- Who will own the Writing Portfolios?

- Who will have access to the portfolios?

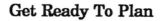

Get Ready To Plan

- Who will be involved in the design of the portfolios and the portfolio system?

- Who will have the major responsibility for over-seeing the planning and for making the kinds of decisions that follow?

- Where and when will planning take place?

Set Goals

- What are the purposes of the portfolios?

- What do you want students to be able to do?

- Will the portfolios be used for writing instruction or assessment or both?

Decide What, Who and When

- What type of portfolio will it be? Work in progress?...best work?...a combination?... private?...one that passes to the next grade?

- When will portfolio use begin?

- Which classes will do portfolios?

Survey Current Writing Instruction

- How will portfolios fit in with the present writing curriculum and instruction?

- Does portfolio use complement current practices?

- Will something need to be changed? What?

The Writing Portfolio

Choose Containers and Contents

- What will the Writing Portfolios look like?

- What will go in the portfolios?

- What are the limits for contents?

- Who will select things?

- What are the criteria for selection?

- Who will set the criteria?

Answer Assessment Questions

- Will the portfolios be used for writing assessment? How?

- How will individual pieces of writing be evaluated? What will be the criteria?

- How will the whole portfolio be evaluated? What will be the criteria?

- Who will do the assessing?

- What form will student self-evaluation take?

- Who will develop the criteria for evaluating pieces and/or the portfolio?

- Is assessment tied to portfolio goals?

- What will you do with assessment results?

selection?

criteria?

Limits?

Assessment?

Self-evaluation?

...go

Design A Management System

- How are selections made?

- How often are selections made?

- How are portfolios handled?

- How are portfolios stored?

- How, when, and how often are student reflections done?

- What kind of time is allotted for review, selecting, revising, reflecting?

- Will teachers, parents, peers review portfolios? How?

- How will portfolios be shared?

- Will students and teachers conference about portfolios? How and when?

- How are records kept on portfolio use, writing growth, achievement?

- What happens to the portfolios at the end of the class or year?

Plan For Parents

- How will parents be involved?

- How will parents be informed about the portfolios?

- Will parents participate in evaluation? If so, how will this happen?

- How will teachers and students report to parents about portfolio use and writing growth and achievement?

BEFORE YOU BEGIN

Checklist

___ **Does the classroom have the kind of climate where portfolios can succeed?**

___ **Who will own the portfolios?**

___ **Who will take part in the design of the portfolios and the system for using them?**

___ **What are the portfolio purposes?**

___ **What type of portfolios?**

___ **Which classes will do them?**

___ **When will we begin?**

___ **How will the portfolios work and fit with the ongoing writing instruction and curriculum?**

___ **What will the portfolios look like?**

___ **What will go in them?**

___ **How will the portfolios be used for assessment?**

___ **Has a management system and timeline been planned?**

___ **How will parents be involved?**

GETTING STARTED WITH WRITING PORTFOLIOS

THE PORTFOLIO JOURNEY

1. Do plenty of writing.
2. Introduce the portfolio concept to students.
3. Agree on the purposes for Writing Portfolios.
4. Make working portfolios.
5. Collect and save.
6. Introduce the portfolio concept to parents.
7. Train students to reflect.
8. Design and create Writing Portfolios.
9. Make management decisions.
10. Make selections for the Portfolio.
11. Self-reflect on selections.
12. Organize the portfolios.
13. Gather reflections from others.
14. Teacher review portfolios.
15. Hold conferences.
16. Repeat above steps.

You've prepared and planned as much as you can. And now you're ready to actually start creating and using Writing Portfolios. As you do so, remember this advice:

- **Keep it simple.** Don't get into a system so complex that it overwhelms or confuses you and the students. Start small—you can always add or expand later.

- **Take your time.** Avoid rushing into a portfolio system or moving too fast. Allow time for each step of the process.

- **Keep an open mind.** Things won't always work the way you've planned. Better ways of proceeding will pop up as you go along. Be open to making needed adaptations.

- **Enjoy.** The process of working with Writing Portfolios is challenging and rewarding. Relax and enjoy it.

Since no two classrooms are alike, no two portfolio approaches will be exactly alike, so there is not any exact formula for you to follow as you take the starting steps. The pages that follow offer a suggested plan of steps for getting Writing Portfolios started in your classroom. Let this plan serve as a general map for the journey you're about to start.

1. DO PLENTY OF WRITING

The processes involved in building and using Writing Portfolios can only truly start if students are using the writing process and creating a good quantity and variety of pieces of writing.

Your students need not be fully accomplished at all steps of the writing process, but they should be working with them. So if writing is not a frequent occurrence in your classroom or if students have not been instructed in the writing process, this is the place to start.

Of course, this first step toward using Writing Portfolios is very much an ongoing one. Writing must continue throughout the steps that follow in order to have the material that keeps the portfolio process going.

The section of this book on pages 28–37 focuses on teaching the writing process. In it is found a teacher's review of the process, a kid's guide to the process, a list of kinds of writing for students to try and many suggestions for teaching writing.

2. INTRODUCE THE PORTFOLIO CONCEPT TO STUDENTS

Share the portfolio concept with your students. The best way to do this is to show them some real life portfolios. Invite an artist, photographer, architect or writer to bring a portfolio into your classroom. Better yet, invite all four. Create a portfolio of your own to show your students. And, if some are available to you, show portfolios created by other children. As you look at portfolios together, discuss:

- what's in them
- what they show (the person's best work, different kinds or styles of work the person can do or has done, some accomplishments, important pieces of work, the processes used to do the work, the person's favorite pieces, the way the person's work or abilities have changed over time, something about who the person is, etc.)
- what the portfolio purpose is
- what's involved in making one
- whether a portfolio contains **all** of a person's work (and why or why not)
- how the creator might decide what to put into the portfolio
- what the purpose of the portfolio seems to be

Introduce students to real portfolios created by real people.

Talk with students specifically about portfolios that primarily contain writing—their appearance, contents or purposes, what they might show or accomplish, how they could be used. Discuss the idea of creating their own Writing Portfolios. Together, think about the kinds of decisions that would need to be made before they actually begin making portfolios.

3. AGREE ON PORTFOLIO PURPOSES

One of the first decisions about the Writing Portfolios is the reason for doing them. Once students understand the portfolio concept, it is time to involve them in making decisions about the portfolio purposes.

Work together on this, combining your goals with their suggestions to make a list of Writing Portfolio purposes for this particular class. (See pages 19–21.) If your school, district or state has required portfolio purposes, the final list will need to incorporate these.

The choice of purposes for your Writing Portfolios is a decision that is crucial to all the other parts of the process, so take your time. Give students several days to think about this. Or make an initial list and come back several days later to rethink and revise. However you go about it, allow enough time to discuss this thoroughly, so that students and teacher agree upon and understand the purposes.

Once the purposes are decided, write them down and keep them visible. You might post them somewhere in the classroom and/or make copies for students to keep inside their Working Portfolios.

Take time to agree on purposes... then make sure they're clear to students.

The purpose of the artist's portfolio is to show a variety of styles and mediums.

LANDSCAPE   PORTRAIT   STILL LIFE

4. MAKE WORKING PORTFOLIOS

Throughout the process of getting started on Writing Portfolios, it is important to keep discussing the concept and the process with your students. Their understanding of portfolios will grow with each day and each new step.

Talk with students about the idea that a final or showcase portfolio doesn't include all of a writer's work. This will lead to their creating of Working Portfolios or Work Folders that can be used to collect and save pieces of writing and other work related to writing.

Give students time and materials for making their Working Portfolios. These need not be fancy. Simple file folders, small boxes or folders made of sturdy construction paper will do. Just make sure the containers are large and sturdy enough to hold all the many pieces they'll collect.

Some students like to organize Working Portfolios by creating different sections such as: Finished Pieces, Work in Progress, Ideas for Writing, Illustrations, etc. You might encourage each student to decide whether and how she or he would like to organize sections of the Working Portfolio.

Since Working Portfolios generally collect a lot of "stuff," a list of contents is helpful. In some classes, students staple a page inside the front of the folder where they can keep a running list of "What's In Here." Each time they put something into the Working Portfolio, they jot down what it is and perhaps the date they filed it.

The Working Portfolio is a treasure chest of good stuff for possible use in the Writing Portfolio.

What's In My Working Portfolio

10/14 — POEM - "The Rusty Nail"

10/19 — Web of Ideas - Halloween

10/20 — Outline for "Spooky Tale"

10/22 — Halloween tale - "A Night To Forget"

11/2 — Alliterative sentences

11/4 — Cassette tape - Reading of limericks

11/7 — Original limericks

11/12 — My response to "Island of the Blue Dolphins"

5. COLLECT AND SAVE

Here's another step that keeps going throughout the year or duration of the class. As students do writing or related activities, they keep adding to the Working Portfolios.

Make a list with students of the kinds of things they could collect as possible contents for their own Writing Portfolios. The guidelines and suggested portfolio contents on pages 46–58 can help you with this. Your group may want to develop its own guidelines for collecting. As students discuss what to save, keep reminding them of the agreed–upon portfolio purposes so that they can think about what kinds of contents will serve to meet those goals.

It isn't necessary to keep all writing, but many classes do. Some groups find it too cumbersome to keep and store everything. Also, if everything stays in this folder, there's little writing to send home. You and your students can decide how to work this. In many classrooms, both students and teachers make choices about what to collect in the Working Portfolio. Often peers, parents and other interested folks within or outside the school setting suggest that something be kept.

If a student wants to keep something in the Working Portfolio and take it home, the copy machine can solve the problem of a piece of work that needs to be in two places at one time. Or a student may take something home to share with parents and bring it back the next day. Whenever something is taken out of the Working Portfolio, the student might leave a note that it has been taken. Most teachers warn against letting students take the whole portfolio home before the end of the year.

It's better to save now and not need it later than to want it later and not have saved it!

©1994 by Incentive Publications, Inc., Nashville, TN.

6. INTRODUCE THE PORTFOLIO CONCEPT TO PARENTS

When students have begun to collect and save work in the Working Portfolios, the time is right for informing parents about the beginnings of your portfolio process. They'll hear their children talk about portfolios and they may notice that fewer samples of writing are coming home from school. It's a good time to give them an introduction to the concept of Writing Portfolios.

This introduction can be done in many ways. You might describe the process at a scheduled Open House or through a regular newsletter. Or you might send home a special letter telling them about the portfolio plans in your classroom.

At this time, it may not be necessary to describe all the details of your Writing Portfolio use. Later on, you'll have more opportunities to share the portfolios and involve parents in portfolio evaluation, if you wish. For now, the main objective is just to let them know what will be happening in the next few weeks or months.

The opposite page gives an example of a letter that introduces parents to the Writing Portfolios being started in one classroom.

October 15

Dear Parents:

As a part of the writing experience and instruction in our classroom, students will soon be creating individual **WRITING PORTFOLIOS**. They have just begun to learn about what portfolios are. We have looked at several examples of professional portfolios used to show the work or abilities of a writer, an architect, a designer and a photographer. We've discussed the concept of creating and using portfolios in our own classroom. Together, the students and I have decided to use Writing Portfolios to help students improve their writing and to involve students in the processes of evaluating their own writing achievement and growth.

At this time, we are just beginning the first steps towards our Writing Portfolios. Each student has made a Working Portfolio to collect all kinds of work related to writing. This means that not all of the writing samples your child generates will be coming home. Many will be saved in the Working Portfolio by the student or by me. You too may recommend a piece of writing be kept in the Working Portfolio.

For the next several weeks, we will be doing lots of writing and saving. The students will also be learning how to reflect on and evaluate their own writing. Later on, students will be ready to select writing samples to move into their Writing Portfolios. When these showcase portfolios are ready, students will be sharing them with you and asking you to respond to them.

For now, you can help by encouraging your child to bring to school for including in the Working Portfolios any special pieces of writing done at home, favorite pieces of literature, or any ideas or treasures that might motivate writing.

We'll keep you posted on our Writing Portfolio progress!

Sincerely,

Mr. Glen Marsh
Roosevelt School

Model and teach self-reflection before asking students to do it.

These words in your story were really scary!

What kind of writing is hardest for me? Why?

I like the way you ended your essay with a question. It showed that this topic has no easy answers.

What would I change about this poem?

I notice that most of the sentences are very long. I need to put in some shorter ones.

What is good about this writing?

Which words are really powerful or descriptive?

This is my favorite writing because it makes people laugh.

7. TRAIN STUDENTS TO REFLECT

The single element of the portfolio process that produces the most growth for students is the element of self-reflection. With Writing Portfolios, this is the act of thinking or writing analytically about their own writing. Most students have never been asked to do this and need to be taught how. If your students have not had this experience before, make sure they begin to learn and practice reflecting on writing **before they actually select elements for their Writing Portfolios.**

Students learn to reflect on their own writing and the writing of others by watching the teacher model reflection, by learning the kinds of questions to ask and by doing it themselves. The sections of this book that deal with reflection, pages 114–139, provide details, forms and examples to help you begin training students in the art of reflecting.

Don't wait to start on this. The more practice students have on reflecting, the more growth-producing will be their experiences with their Writing Portfolios.

8. DESIGN AND CREATE PORTFOLIOS

The next step is to have students begin to make the actual Writing Portfolio to showcase particular pieces. Depending on their experience with the writing and reflecting processes, different classes are ready for this at different times. It may be several months before your students are ready to move pieces into the showcase portfolio.

The only rule about how long to wait before you start making and selecting for the actual portfolio is this one: start when you and your students are ready. Ready means that enough time has passed to allow students to create and save several pieces of writing and to practice reflecting on writing.

When you are ready, provide students with plenty of time to plan, design and create their portfolios. If students can do this over a period of a week or two, they'll have a chance to gather the materials they need and to truly express themselves in the design of their Writing Portfolios.

Pages 42–45 provide suggestions and ideas for choosing and designing containers. Page 45 gives suggestions for personalizing portfolios.

If you haven't already started one, don't forget to make your own Writing Portfolio, too. Do this right along with your students. You'll get good ideas from them!

9. MAKE MANAGEMENT DECISIONS

After (or during) the time that the Writing Portfolios are created and before the first works are selected to move into them, the students and teacher together must make many decisions about just how this is all going to work. It is crucial that students take an active part in making decisions about the portfolio system. Take time to reach agreement on management concerns and details of operating such as these:

So many decisions to make!

- Where and how will the portfolios be stored?
- Who owns the portfolios?
- Who will have access to the portfolio besides the student, and under what conditions?
- How often will selections be made?
- What kinds of selections will be made at each selection time?
- How will the type of selection be decided?
- Who will make the selections?
- How many items will be selected at one time?
- Is there a limit on the total number of selections to be moved into the portfolio?
- What are the criteria for selection?
- How will the criteria be decided? By whom?
- Can something be removed from the Writing Portfolio once it's been put in there?
- How will self-reflections be done?
- How often will self-reflections be done?
- Will anyone else review or reflect on some or all of the selections? Who?
- What kind of time will be available for making selections and reflections?

No two systems of management will be exactly alike...because no two classrooms are exactly alike.

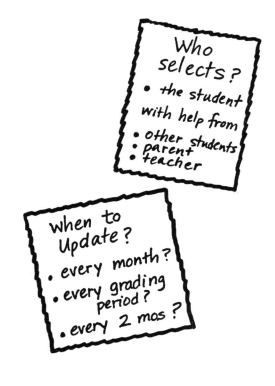

Who selects?
• the student with help from
• other students
• parent
• teacher

when to Update?
• every month?
• every grading period?
• every 2 mos?

Sharing Portfolios
• Peer Groups?
• Parent Night?
• Partners?

End of Year
• Pass along to the next grade?
• Take it home?

Who owns the Portfolio?

- How and when will the portfolios be updated?
- How will the teacher review the portfolios?
- Will portfolios or their contents be graded or evaluated? How and by whom?
- What are the criteria for evaluation?
- How, when and where will portfolios be shared?
- What will happen to the portfolios at the end of the year?

These are certainly not the only questions to be answered. You can add or subtract from the list as you become aware of questions that need to be answered for your group.

Be aware that no two management systems will be exactly alike. Nor should they be. The procedures you settle upon **must be designed specifically for your classroom and your students' needs**. It rarely works for a class to try to "transplant" a portfolio system from another place. You may certainly glean and borrow ideas from others, but you must make it your own. And if a great idea doesn't fit your classroom, don't hesitate to throw it out.

So that you can get an idea of how some different classrooms have designed systems for using their Writing Portfolios, see pages 94–97 for some sample timelines and management systems.

10. MAKE SELECTIONS

When raw material has been gathered and the workings of the system have been ironed out, the first selections can be made for the Writing Portfolios (or Showcase Portfolios). This is an exciting part of the process—one that most students dive into eagerly. It is much more than just making a choice. To do the selecting, students engage in many valuable processes. As they go through their portfolios, they get deeply involved in reviewing, revising, scrutinizing, analyzing and comparing works. They use a variety of thinking and decision making skills. This step of making portfolio selections is therefore a very important learning activity and is worthy of plenty of time and support to students.

Who selects? The final selection should be left to the portfolio owner. However, many students may need help with the selecting process, particularly in the beginning. The goal is to nurture writers to the place where they are confident to make their own selections. On the way to this goal, writers can receive valuable support and input from peers, the teacher and others. What is helpful are sensitive responses that encourage and assist, without telling the writer what "should" be chosen.

When to select? This will vary in different classrooms. You may decide that selections will be made weekly, monthly, quarterly or on any other schedule. Choose a plan that works for your classroom. Whatever the schedule, it is important that the students know the timing. They need to be given time to make choices and they need to know how much time they'll have.

Criteria for selection must be clear to the student.

What to select? What are the criteria for selection? Are there specific kinds of writing that are to be chosen? These criteria need to be agreed upon before selection begins. If the choice is more open, such as "Choose three pieces of writing for your Writing Portfolio," then students may need help setting some guidelines of their own. For instance, they may consider choosing a piece that they really like, one that that shows how well they can do a kind of writing, one that centers on a special interest or one that shows something done especially well or demonstrates a goal met.

How many to select? The number of selections will vary according to student needs and portfolio purposes. Some groups begin with one selection, others select three or more at a time. It is a good idea to have a limit on the number of pieces in the portfolio. Too few may not give a representative sampling of a student's writing ability or growth. But too many will make it time consuming and cumbersome to review and evaluate the portfolio. You might consider a total in the range of 6–15 pieces over a year.

Labeling Each piece selected for the Writing Portfolio should have a comment or label that identifies the criteria for its selection or tells why it was chosen. For instance:

This is the best writing I did this month.

This piece shows how my writing has improved.

This selection shows a piece of writing through all stages of the writing process.

This is a piece I had the most trouble writing.

I chose this to show that I'm good at poetry.

11. SELF–REFLECT

Each of the selections that a student chooses to showcase in the Writing Portfolio will have some label noting why the piece was chosen. In addition, most or all of the selections should be accompanied by some kind of self–reflection.

The form of the reflection will, of course, vary according to the age and ability of the writer, the purposes of the portfolio, the criteria for selection, the type of selection, the class requirements and other factors. It may be as simple as "This is my favorite piece of writing because it has lots of funny words and makes me laugh." Or it may be as complex and detailed as a page–long discussion of how the piece shows the author's development and growth as a writer.

There are limitless possibilities of ways for students to reflect on their writing. Probably no two reflections have ever been quite the same. There is no one right or best way. The important thing is that students are given the opportunity to think about their writing, consider themselves as writers and do some sort of analysis of the process or the piece.

A later section of this book focuses specifically on the topic of reflecting on writing. (See pages 114–139). It will give you direction for teaching students to reflect, examples of several types of reflection, sample forms and techniques for reflecting and examples of student self–reflections.

12. ORGANIZE PORTFOLIOS

An important part of preparing the portfolio for review by others is the process of getting it organized. Give students time to label and sequence items in the portfolio and to attach the reflections to corresponding pieces. Each time the Writing Portfolio is prepared for review, the student should include an up-to-date Contents Page. This page itemizes and briefly describes what is in the portfolio. See pages 52–53 for more details on the Contents Page.

13. GATHER REFLECTIONS FROM OTHERS

Writers of all abilities and ages can benefit greatly from the reflections of others. The process of receiving responses from others benefits not only the writer, but the reader as well. Both learn something about effective writing and about the processes of evaluation.

Schedule the time and the opportunities for students to gather reflections on their writing from others—such as peers, parents, friends outside school, teachers or other school personnel. This is not necessary to do for every selection in the Writing Portfolio. But it certainly is valuable to do sometimes. My recommendation would be that each Writing Portfolio contain at least one or two reflections contributed by someone other than the writer. These may be reflections on individual pieces of writing or on the portfolio as a whole.

See pages 138–139 for ideas about gathering responses to Writing Portfolios from parents, peers and others.

14. (TEACHER) REVIEW PORTFOLIOS

When the students' selections are made, self-reflections are included and reflections have been gathered from others, the Writing Portfolios are ready for teacher review. The teacher reviews Writing Portfolios for these purposes:

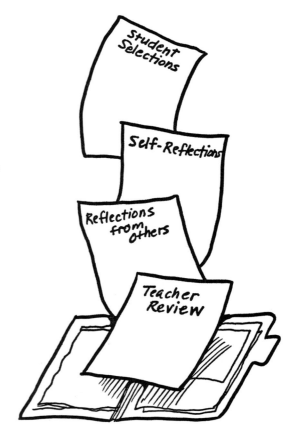

- to get a look at who the student is as a writer at this time

- to gain a picture of how the student evaluates her or his own writing at this time

- to identify the writer's strengths and weaknesses (i.e., how various parts of the writing process and writing techniques are used and handled, which areas present problems, how the writer handles problems, what instructional intervention is needed, etc.)

- to record observations, questions or concerns to discuss with the student at a conference

Keeping notes

When reviewing student Writing Portfolios, be sure to keep good records for use in conferences or for future use in evaluating student achievement and progress. Keep notes descriptive, simple and clear. Your notes might include:

- a list of what the portfolio contains
- a few descriptive comments about the portfolio or particular pieces
- a few strengths and needs you identify
- 1 or 2 specific points you want to make when talking to the student
- 1 or 2 possible goals for the student

WRITING PORTFOLIO REVIEW

Student _Samantha G._   Teacher _Ms. Alvarez_   Date

PORTFOLIO CONTENTS

Snowflake Rhyme
"I Can" Photo Essay
Picture-Web for animal description
"The Animal I'd Love" description

STRENGTHS and NEEDS

descriptive, winter, snowy words
many examples for essay
not clear or specific on description
some what lacking in voice

SELF-REFLECTIONS

Very general and alike

TEACHING POINTS

★ Show how descriptive words car
   clearer picture of animal
★ ask questions to help reflection
   to the piece

GOALS

★ Try another description that gives
   picture to reader.
★ Say something about the piece of u
   special when reflecting.

Teachers develop different methods for keeping records of their portfolio reviews. One way is to create a form such as one of these for recording comments. This can be kept in the Teacher's Assessment Portfolio and retrieved when it's time for a conference.

TEACHER REVIEW of PORTFOLIO

STUDENT _Shana Adams_

Date _November 12_

OBSERVATIONS	STRENGTHS and NEEDS
✱ 5 selections - good variety. Chose one because she found it hard	✱ takes risks well
	✱ strong organization
	✱ good attention to detail
✱ future Problem Solving piece very interesting and unusual	✱ transitions are rough
	✱ weak dialogue
Written analysis/verbal analysis show great self confidence	✱ little attention to spelling & punctuation
	✱ needs help identifying Problems
✱ reflection focuses only on strengths	GOALS
	1 - Use dialogue more fully
	2 - Use peer editor to help with mechanics
	3 - identify - reflect on one need

Date _January 30_

OBSERVATIONS	STRENGTHS and NEEDS
✱ poem groups	✱ clear outlines
✱ narrative outline	✱ improved dialogue use
✱ jokes book	✱ good voice particularly
✱ photo essay	with photo essay
✱ narrative with dialogue	✱ good sense of humor shows in writing
✱ talked more about what she's learning	✱ problems with paragraphing
✱ reflections include more aspects of process	✱ revisions are hurried
✱ more enthusiasm for writing	GOALS
	1 - get revision response from 2 people
	2 - try 2 new forms

Notes such as these serve as a valuable guide for your conferences with students. Even if you're not holding a conference each time you review the portfolio, your collected observations build good assessment data.

The portfolio conference is one of the best examples there is of an effective student–teacher partnership in learning.

15. HOLD CONFERENCES

A Writing Portfolio conference yields many important benefits for both the teacher and the student.

The **student** gets a chance to share a prized re-presentation of self and accomplishments. Portfolio conferences strengthen students' pride and ownership in their work, provide a forum for them to talk about themselves as writers and expand opportunities for self-evaluation. Students get to elaborate orally on what they've been thinking and learning about their writing. In addition, the conference supplies a way for each student to receive some direct and personal response, insight and instruction from the teacher.

The **teacher** is provided with more information and insight about the student's writing and thinking. The portfolio conference lets the teacher hear from the student what is important, what is needed, what pleases and displeases and how the portfolio process is working. It also gives the teacher a time and place to give personalized support and affirmation.

The main role of the teacher in the conference is to listen.

Conferencing plays a major part in the portfolio process. If you could eavesdrop on a good writing portfolio conference, you would observe in action one of the best examples there is of an effective student–teacher partnership in learning.

Conference Guidelines Before beginning the first conferences, keep in mind:

- Students should know about conferences ahead of time so they can adequately prepare. Inform each student of the date, time and place, the purpose of the conference, what to expect and what they need to do to get ready for the conference.

- Conferences must be student–centered. This means that the writer is in charge of the conference and does most of the talking. It is a time for the writer to show, share, explain the Writing Portfolio to the teacher.

- The teacher's role in the conference is one that is supportive and non–judgmental. The goal is to praise and encourage.

- Listen to the student. You will learn from the conference what you could not learn from the portfolio review alone.

- The Writing Portfolio conference is a place and time to do far more than review or discuss individual pieces of writing. Use this setting to reinforce both the writing process and the portfolio process.

✔ Inform students ahead of time

✔ Let the student do most of the talking

✔ Praise – don't judge

✔ Listen

✔ Emphasize the process

Conference goals What do you wish to accomplish with Writing Portfolio conferences? Think about your goals before you begin the conferences. Deciding these will help you know how to proceed with conferencing. Share goals and procedures with the students.

As students gain experience in portfolio use and conferencing, you might ask them to set their own goals for the Writing Portfolio conference.

Writing Portfolio Conference
TEACHER'S GOALS

★ Listen to the student talk about the Writing Portfolio

★ Reinforce writing strengths

★ Reinforce self-evaluation strengths

★ Teach something

★ Help the student set goals

listen

sample goals...

Writing Portfolio Conference
STUDENT'S GOALS

★ Share my writing and my portfolio with the teacher

★ Tell what I think and feel about my portfolio

★ Show the teacher how good I am at using dialogue in my writing

★ Ask for help with story beginnings

★ Set goals for next month's writing

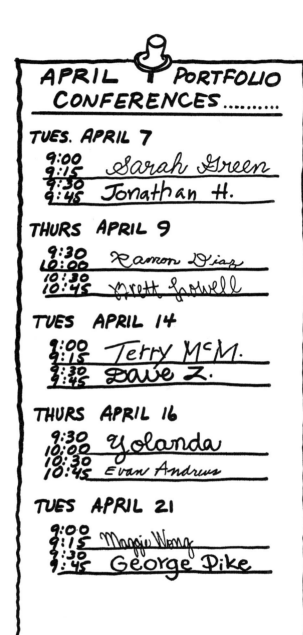

APRIL PORTFOLIO CONFERENCES ....

TUES. APRIL 7
9:00 Sarah Green
9:15
9:30 Jonathan H.
9:45

THURS APRIL 9
9:30 Ramon Diaz
10:00
10:30 Brett Howell
10:45

TUES APRIL 14
9:00 Terry McM.
9:15
9:30 Dave Z.
9:45

THURS APRIL 16
9:30 Yolanda
10:00
10:30 Evan Andrews
10:45

TUES APRIL 21
9:00 Maggie Wong
9:15
9:30 George Pike
9:45

Scheduling conferences The time, place, length and frequency of your Writing Portfolio conferences will all depend on your classroom procedures and needs. Every portfolio classroom does it differently. As you make decisions about scheduling, consider:

When? Conferences must be held when the teacher can devote time and full attention to one student. Many teachers do this during a time when students are doing writing and revisions, independent reading or other individual work. Some hold conferences during recesses or other break times. A teacher may plan for all the conferences in one week or may fit in one or two a day over a period of two to three weeks.

How Long? An ideal portfolio conference might last 10–15 minutes. It's wonderful when a conference of this length can happen at least once or twice a year, if not more. Mini-conferences of five minutes are used by many teachers when schedules don't permit longer times.

How Often? This varies widely. Conferences are such valuable learning experiences for teacher and students that twice a year is a recommended minimum. You might choose to conference once each grading period, once a month, every two months, at the end of each semester, or whenever you can fit it in.

Conferencing is not a must every time students update Writing Portfolios, though some type of sharing is important. In high schools and middle schools where teachers cannot possibly conference often with the large number of students, many arrange to hold conferences with two or three students at a time or teach students to conduct peer conferences.

<u>Conducting the conference</u> Here is an example of how the conference might proceed:

1. Let the student hold the portfolio and hand you pieces which he or she wants to share with you.

2. Ask the student to share the portfolio with you. You might begin with:

   What do you want to share first?

3. Continue to ask questions that help the student keep thinking, reflecting and sharing, such as:

   Tell me why you included this.

   Show me your favorite piece. Why is it your favorite?

   What do you feel you are doing especially well?

   Could you read a sentence or a phrase that shows some of your best writing?

   How do you feel about your writing?

   What do you think are the strengths of this piece (or of all the writing)?

   Which of these pieces was the hardest to write?

   How has your writing changed?

   Are you having trouble with anything?

   Is there anything you need help with?

   What do you like best about your writing in this piece?

What are you doing especially well?

I'm getting ideas in the right order!

4. As the student talks about the portfolio, respond with praise and encouragement. This is a good chance to use and reinforce the reflective techniques you've been teaching. When possible, agree with the student's self-evaluation of strengths or improvements. As you go along, point out good writing techniques and other strengths in the writing or in the student's self-evaluation:

The use of this phrase is really effective.

Yes, you used questions well. I liked that too!

There's a nice variety in the lengths of your sentences.

5. During the course of the conference, find a way to teach one or two things to the student. Point out a possible change that would strengthen the writing, show the student a new technique that might work in a piece, or help with a problem the student identifies.

6. Help the student to analyze the portfolio process as well as individual pieces by asking questions such as:

How did you go about choosing these pieces?

What have you learned from doing your portfolio?

Would you do anything differently next time you make selections for your Writing Portfolio?

7. Before the conference is ended, ask the student to set a few goals to work toward for future writing. Help the student choose manageable, realistic goals.

Keeping records on conferences—Since you gain so many insights and understandings as students share their Writing Portfolios with you, it is crucial that you maintain clear records on each conference. Keep conference notes on each student in your **Teacher's Assessment Portfolio** or a loose-leaf notebook.

Many teachers develop forms for recording conference insights. This can be combined on a form with the notes from a pre-conference review of the portfolio. Some teachers like to keep notes about conferences on a class record sheet to cut down on the amount of paper used for record-keeping. The best record-keeping processes and forms are always the ones created for your unique needs and situation. These examples can help you create your own.

WRITING PORTFOLIO CONFERENCE RECORD

Student Nicholas Mc Nielson

DATE	PORTFOLIO ELEMENTS	STRENGTHS & NEEDS	SELF-ANALYSIS	STUDENT COMMENTS	GOALS	COMMENTS
10-29	-Reading response -Essay -Argument -Advertisement -Process Package for Space Fantasy -Reflections -Collection of ideas for future writing	Strong titles + beginnings Strong voice Effective sentence structure Strong ideas Pieces weaken near end Repetitive ideas short on backup details in essay	able to focus on writing techniques can describe process well realizes need for more substance to back ideas & arguments	"I start out strong then fizzle" "I repeated the same ideas too much" "I put myself into my writing"	1) Slow down 2) Spend more time gathering ideas and details before writing 3) try another persuasive piece with more reasons behind argument	very promising at identifying his work processes and what he needs to improve

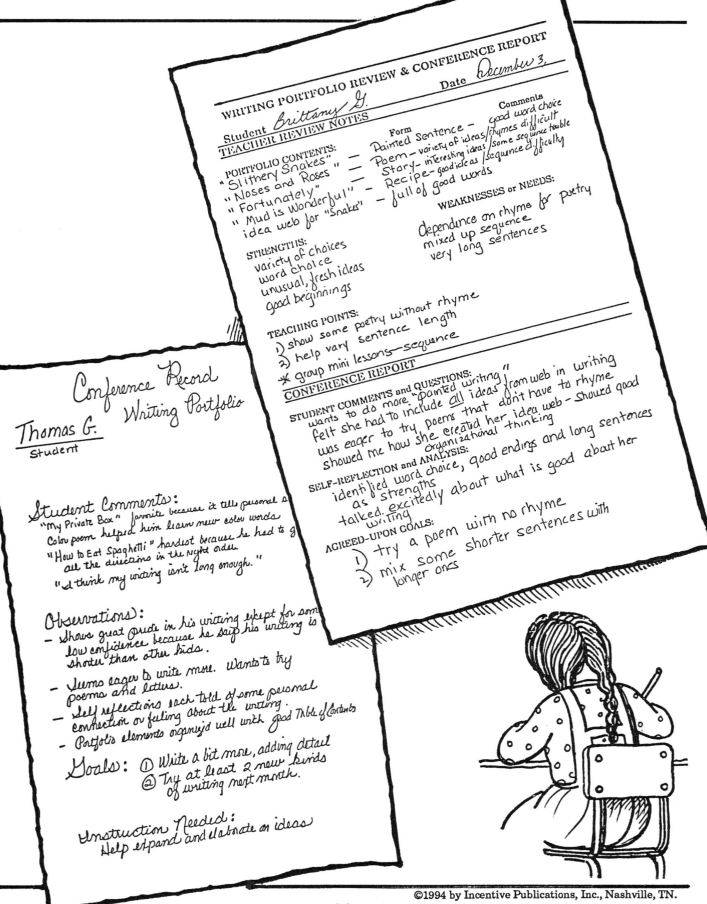

WRITING PORTFOLIO REVIEW & CONFERENCE REPORT

Date December 3

Student Brittany G.

TEACHER REVIEW NOTES

PORTFOLIO CONTENTS:
- "Slithery Snakes"
- "Noses and Roses"
- "Fortunately"
- "Mud is Wonderful"
- idea web for "Snakes"

Form — Comments
- Painted Sentence — good word choice
- Poem — variety of ideas/rhymes difficult
- Story — interesting ideas/some sequence trouble
- Recipe — good ideas/sequence difficulty
- full of good words

STRENGTHS:
variety of choices
word choice
unusual, fresh ideas
good beginnings

WEAKNESSES or NEEDS:
dependence on rhyme for poetry
mixed up sequence
very long sentences

TEACHING POINTS:
1) show some poetry without rhyme
2) help vary sentence length
✱ group mini lessons—sequence

CONFERENCE REPORT

STUDENT COMMENTS and QUESTIONS:
wants to do more "painted writing"
felt she had to include all ideas from web in writing
was eager to try poems that don't have to rhyme
showed me how she created her idea web — should good
organizational thinking

SELF-REFLECTION and ANALYSIS:
identified word choice, good endings and long sentences
as strengths
talked excitedly about what is good about her
writing

AGREED-UPON GOALS:
1) try a poem with no rhyme
2) mix some shorter sentences with
longer ones

Conference Record
Writing Portfolio

Thomas G.
Student

Student Comments:
"My Private Box" favorite because it tell personal s...
Color poem helped him learn new color words
"How to Eat Spaghetti" hardest because he had to g...
all the directions in the right order.
"I think my writing isn't long enough."

Observations:
- Shows great pride in his writing except for som...
  low confidence because he says his writing is
  shorter than other kids.
- Seems eager to write more. Wants to try
  poems and letters.
- Self reflections each told of some personal
  connection or feeling about the writing.
- Portfolio elements organized well with good Table of Contents

Goals: ① Write a bit more, adding detail
② Try at least 2 new kinds
of writing next month.

Instruction Needed:
Help expand and elaborate on ideas

SAMPLE PORTFOLIO SYSTEM

★ Students write and save writing in Working Portfolio.

★ Twice a year, 2–3 selections are made. Students self-reflect, conference with teacher and share portfolios with parents and peers.

★ At end-of-year, they write or dictate an evaluation of the whole portfolio and the portfolio process.

SAMPLE PORTFOLIO SYSTEM

★ Accumulate writing.

★ When 10–15 samples are collected, students choose 1–3 to move to the Writing Portfolio.

★ ...ch selection, the writer ... Why I Chose This, What it ...at I Learned.

★ ...r comments from ...er.

★ ...rtfolio with the ...als.

★ ... 2 months.

SAMPLE PORTFOLIO SYSTEM

★ From Sept–Dec students write, collect and learn to reflect on writing.

★ Students make 4 portfolio selections in January and in March. They self-reflect on each and hold conferences with the teacher.

★ In May, students review and update portfolios as they wish. Then they write an evaluation of the whole portfolio and process.

SAMPLE PORTFOLIO SYSTEM

★ Learn about writing portfolios. Write and collect.

★ 3 times a year, choose 1–2 samples for the Writing Portfolio.

★ Each time, tell: *Why I Chose This, What is Good About This Writing,* and *What I Need to Improve.*

★ Each time, share portfolio with someone else. Get written or oral comments.

★ At end of year, write or tell: *How I've Changed as a Writer* and *What I Learned from Doing a Writing Portfolio.*

PORTFOLIO SYSTEM SAMPLE

★ Write and save.

★ At end of each quarter, students select 1 piece with help from peers, parent, teacher.

★ Students reflect on each piece.

★ Conferences are held each quarter with teacher alone or in small groups.

SAMPLE P...

★ During Language Arts block, students read, write, edit, meet with editing groups and revise while teacher holds individual conferences or calls small groups.

★ Whenever a student is ready—he or she makes a few selections for the Writing Portfolio, does self-evaluation of the pieces and portfolio and schedules a conference with the teacher.

...RTFOLIO SYSTEM

★ ...d collect.

★ ...lection is made for ...rding to criteria ...the class.

★ ...each student writes a ...ve letter evaluating the ...nd the process.

★ ...ents move or copy elements into a Pass-Along Writing Portfolio for the district's use.

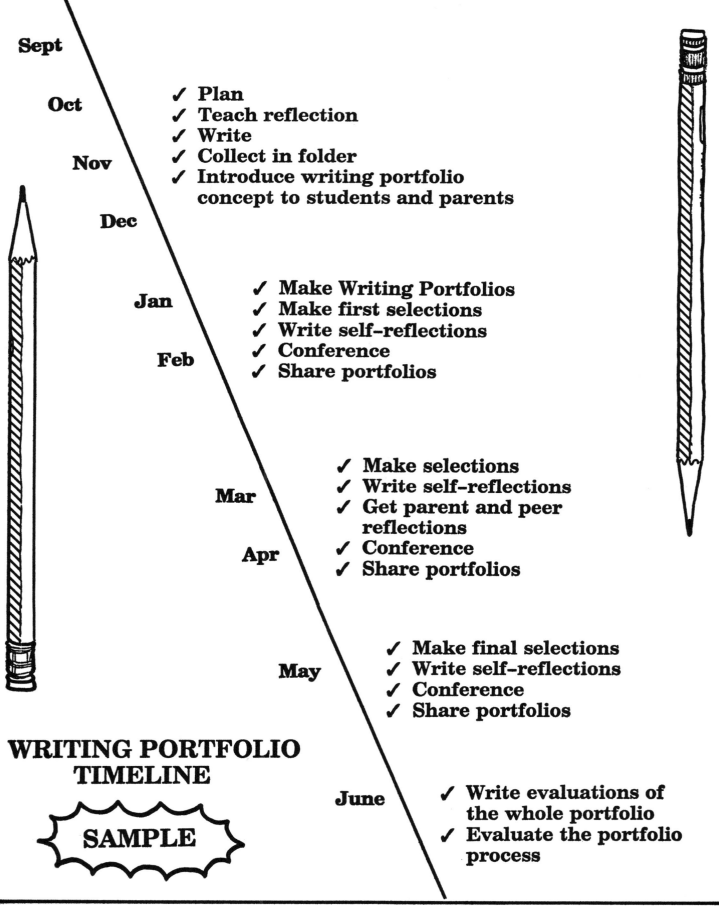

Sept

Oct

✓ **Plan**
✓ **Teach reflection**
✓ **Write**
✓ **Collect in folder**
✓ **Introduce writing portfolio**
   concept to students and parents

Nov

Dec

✓ **Make Writing Portfolios**
✓ **Make first selections**
✓ **Write self–reflections**
✓ **Conference**
✓ **Share portfolios**

Jan

Feb

✓ **Make selections**
✓ **Write self–reflections**
✓ **Get parent and peer**
   reflections
✓ **Conference**
✓ **Share portfolios**

Mar

Apr

✓ **Make final selections**
✓ **Write self–reflections**
✓ **Conference**
✓ **Share portfolios**

May

WRITING PORTFOLIO
TIMELINE

SAMPLE

June

✓ **Write evaluations of**
   the whole portfolio
✓ **Evaluate the portfolio**
   process

WRITING PORTFOLIO TIMELINE

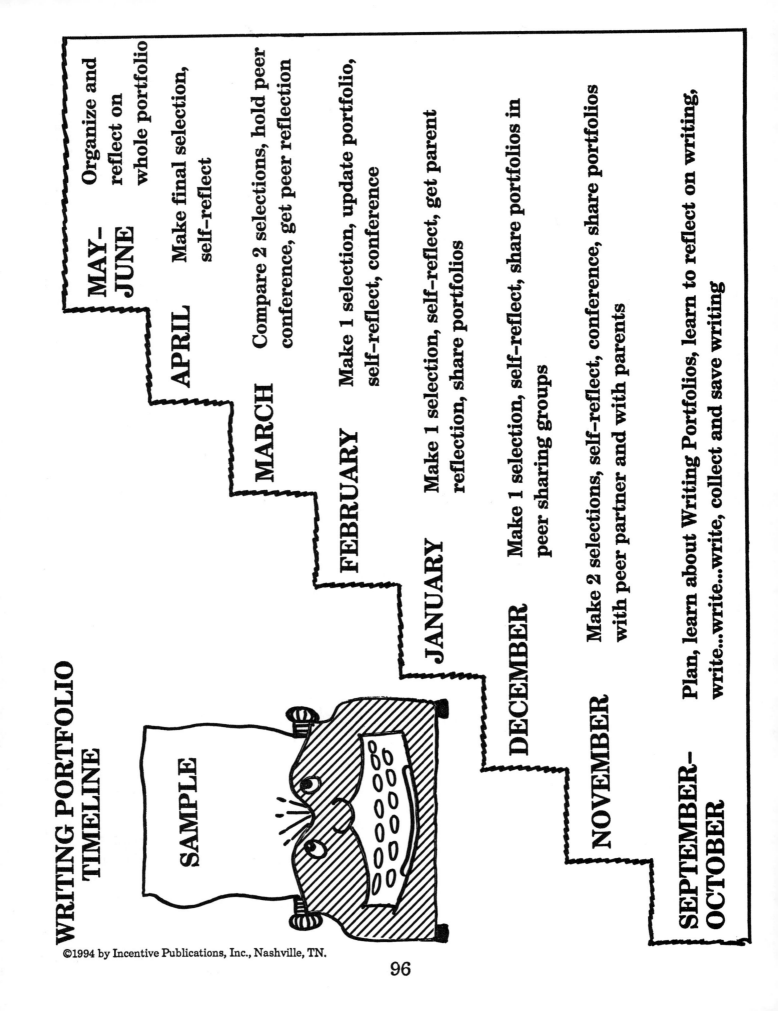

SAMPLE

MAY–JUNE — Organize and reflect on whole portfolio

APRIL — Make final selection, self-reflect

MARCH — Compare 2 selections, hold peer conference, get peer reflection

FEBRUARY — Make 1 selection, update portfolio, self-reflect, conference

JANUARY — Make 1 selection, self-reflect, get parent reflection, share portfolios

DECEMBER — Make 1 selection, self-reflect, share portfolios in peer sharing groups

NOVEMBER — Make 2 selections, self-reflect, conference, share portfolios with peer partner and with parents

SEPTEMBER–OCTOBER — Plan, learn about Writing Portfolios, learn to reflect on writing, write...write...write, collect and save writing

WRITING PORTFOLIO TIMELINE

SAMPLE

SEPTEMBER
WORK ON WRITING PROCESS
MAKE WORK FOLDERS
COLLECT LOTS OF WRITING

OCTOBER
INTRODUCE PORTFOLIO IDEA
MAKE WRITING PORTFOLIOS
MAKE DECISIONS & PLAN
INFORM PARENTS

NOVEMBER
SELECT "FAVORITE PIECE"
SELECT ONE OTHER PIECE
SELF–REFLECT
ORGANIZE PORTFOLIOS
CONFERENCE

DECEMBER
KEEP WRITING AND SAVING
WORK ON WRITING PROCESS
SHARE PORTFOLIOS

JANUARY
SELECT "MOST IMPROVED PIECE"
SELF–REFLECT, PEER–REFLECT
ORGANIZE PORTFOLIOS

FEBRUARY
1 PARENT SELECTION
1 SELF–SELECTION
SELF–REFLECT
PARENT REFLECT
CONFERENCE

MARCH
KEEP WRITING AND SAVING
WORK ON WRITING PROCESS
CLASS PORTFOLIO PARTY

APRIL
SELECT "PROCESS PACKAGE"
SELECT FREE PICK
SELF–REFLECT
CONFERENCE

MAY
REVIEW & UPDATE PORTFOLIOS
*SELECT AND COMPARE 1 "EARLY
PIECE" AND 1 "LATER PIECE"*
ORGANIZE PORTFOLIOS

JUNE
REVIEW PORTFOLIOS
*WRITE METACOGNITIVE LETTERS
EVALUATING PORTFOLIOS*
EVALUATE PORTFOLIO PROCESS

◄----FINAL CONFERENCES----►

KEEPING WRITING PORTFOLIOS GOING

It takes plenty of planning and preparation to get the Writing Portfolio process off the ground. Each of the steps from the beginning interest through the first student selections, reflections and conferences is important to the framework of the portfolio process. Yet the possibilities for student growth and for valuable assessment can only be realized where those first steps are maintained, repeated, refined and expanded.

As the Writing Portfolios are sustained over time, the benefits really begin to be evident. Students and teachers alike get better at identifying and analyzing strengths, difficulties and progress. Self-evaluation abilities grow. Instruction improves. Writing improves. And the sense of ownership and excitement about learning flourish.

UPDATE PORTFOLIOS REGULARLY

Each time students update their portfolios, they grow and improve at using all the portfolio processes. Their selecting, organizing and analyzing skills become more sophisticated. And they gain confidence in their abilities to make decisions and to evaluate their own learning.

Working within your chosen schedule for work with portfolios, make sure that students have regular opportunities to update their Writing Portfolios. First the group must decide on the number of pieces to be selected and the criteria for selection. Then students can get to the exciting work of updating. They can revisit the portfolio, review other collected work, and consider what to keep, change, revise, replace eliminate or add.

The real growth comes when the Writing Portfolios are sustained over time.

CELEBRATE GROWTH

Stop...look...take time to notice what's happening.

What are students learning during the portfolio process? What are you learning?

As you and your students continue "growing" your Writing Portfolios, pay attention to the progress. Celebrate it! Talk with the students about what's happening to them, to the teacher, to the class. Make a list together of growths to celebrate.

KEEP LEARNING

Teaching students how to make and use Writing Portfolios doesn't end when the folders are decorated and the first selections are placed inside it. Some think that once they've gone through all the steps on pages 68-97, they've got the system down—they know how to do it. But that's only the beginning.

As students work with their portfolios, make it part of your plan to continue to share experiences, solve problems together, talk about better ways of doing things, practice reflection and learn more about metacognition. You and your students will learn more every time you put your heads together to share, complain, question, reconsider, celebrate or solve problems.

Keep learning on your own, too. Read, talk with colleagues, attend workshops—to find out more about portfolio use. And don't forget to share with your students the new ideas you discover.

It feels so good to write without being afraid someone is going to criticize me.

I learned to make choices.

The writing doesn't have to be long to be good.

It's Okay to have problems with writing.

I am more proud of my writing now.

the portfolio makes my writing important

I am better at seeing where my strengths are.

The reflections of other kids help make my writing better.

We all have more fun writing than we used to !

Portfolio tasks are not just paperwork.

Portfolios are worth the time— every minute of it.

TAKE THE TIME

Where are we ever going to find the time to do all this?

When many teachers hear the portfolio process described, the clock starts ticking loudly inside their heads and they wonder how they'll ever fit this in with all the other demands of the classroom and curriculum.

Yes, portfolios take time. The valuable skills and processes involved in creating and updating Writing Portfolios can't possibly develop adequately unless students are allowed adequate time to do them thoroughly, without feeling rushed.

So how **do** you find the time? The first step toward answering this question is to look at this list of what students are doing when they do portfolios. Notice... appreciate...think about the learning processes and skills being used and developed.

This is worth the time—every minute of it. This is not just paperwork, or busywork. What students are doing when they prepare portfolios is good stuff. **It is real learning.**

Think of these activities not as something you're **adding** to the curriculum—but as a different way of accomplishing the very writing or language arts goals you know are important for students. Think about learning activities you're doing now that can be incorporated into the portfolio process or that duplicate what is being accomplished through the use of portfolios. Often you'll be able to eliminate a usual activity because portfolios do it better.

How much time does it take? This depends, of course, on your portfolio system, the ages and abilities of your writers, and the structure of your classroom. In many classrooms, portfolio updating just slides right into the normal writing workshop proceedings, with students using their normal writing–editing time to update portfolios.

There are different ways to arrange for the time needed. Here are a few of the ways portfolio updating might be scheduled:

- 30 or 40 minutes every day for two weeks
- one class period a day
- 3–4 days of reading group time
- the language arts time every day for a week
- two whole mornings

Two factors considerably affect the time needed for portfolio use:

1) **The management system**—If you have a simple, well-organized plan for making portfolios work, your use of time for all aspects of the process will be much more efficient.

2) **The amount of student responsibility**—The time problem, particularly for the teacher, will be significantly reduced as students increase in ownership and independence and take greater responsibility for collecting, filing, sharing, analyzing and tasks involved with the Writing Portfolios.

I need time for...

collecting

re-visiting

re-reading

finishing

revising

sorting

comparing

selecting

deleting

condensing

organizing

labeling

reflecting

gathering reflections

analyzing

collaborating

putting together

sharing

INCREASE STUDENT INDEPENDENCE

As students gain more and more experience with the skills and activities involved in keeping Writing Portfolios, they'll gain in ability to take more responsibility for many parts of the process. It is important that the teacher recognizes and permits that independence. Students of all ages can increase their responsibilities. Look for ways to hand over more control to them as soon as they're ready. They can take responsibility for things such as:

- collecting and filing
- storing portfolios
- keeping records of what's in Working Portfolios as well as Writing Portfolios
- setting criteria for selection
- contributing to peer editing groups
- scheduling own conferences
- preparing for conferences
- organizing portfolio materials
- asking for help
- keeping a list of accomplishments or problems
- sharing portfolios

Gradually give students more control over their own portfolios.

Increasing student independence and control increases the growth realized from doing portfolios. It also enhances their pride, ownership, involvement and self esteem. A wonderful fringe benefit is that greater student responsibility saves work for the teacher.

ADJUST WRITING INSTRUCTION

A key part of sustaining the Writing Portfolio process is continuing, adapting and improving the writing instruction in the classroom. This may take place with individuals, small groups or the whole class—but it needs to keep happening on a regular basis.

Portfolio use has many rewarding outcomes. Some of the best ones are the lessons the teacher learns about which particular type of writing instruction students need. This information comes to you in the form of instant feedback from reviewing student Writing Portfolios and listening to students talk about their writing. Pay attention to this feedback. Keep track of what is working, what isn't working and what is needed. Build your writing lessons and activities around this information. Pages 106–110 provide some ideas about how to use what you learn from Writing Portfolios to improve writing instruction.

EVALUATE THE PORTFOLIOS

Evaluation is another critical task involved in sustaining and developing portfolio use and usefulness. In order to provide valuable assessment information this needs to be done carefully and thoughtfully. Student self-reflections give evaluations of individual pieces of writing. It is crucial to also involve them in analyzing their portfolios as a whole. They must also take part in evaluating the processes they've used in developing and using Writing Portfolios in the classroom. (See pages 112–113 and 140–144 for reasons and approaches for evaluating the portfolios and the portfolio process.)

Listen to what students and portfolios can tell about writing instruction.

writing portfolio

Evaluate the whole portfolio, not just the pieces in it.

KEEP GOOD RECORDS

The greatest advantages of portfolio use can be enjoyed when you have a very clear idea of what you're learning from them. If a student's Writing Portfolio and the processes used to produce it are going to help you provide appropriate and needed writing instruction—and if accurate and useful assessment data is to result, there must be a system for keeping good records of what's happening. Clear, meaningful records are valuable to all persons involved in the learning process.

What kinds of records should be kept? How many to keep? How often? Where? Record-keeping can be a nightmare. It can overwhelm you and take the joy out of the whole portfolio process. As you think about designing your own record-keeping system, keep these guidelines in mind:

- Keep records that will build the assessment and instructional data you want to have on each student and/or on the class.

- Make sure your records are adequate. You need enough information to demonstrate what you're trying to show.

- Don't keep anything you don't really need. It's very easy to get overwhelmed by too many forms, records and checklists. So create a record-keeping system that is **simple** and well organized.

- Store records where they are secure and confidential. Take care that students see only own records.

Don't let yourself get buried in checklists and records.

Here are some of the records you might keep:

Anecdotal Notes—As you work with students, take notice of particular characteristics, problems, questions, changes, needs you see in their writing and in their portfolio preparation. Jot down dated notes on a prepared form, stick-on notes or index cards. Drop them into your own assessment folder. Some teachers wander around the classroom with a clipboard full of forms on which they keep a running list of anecdotal notes on each student. These notes will add to the information you gain from reviewing Writing Portfolios and conferencing with students.

Portfolio Review Notes—Keep notes each time you review a Writing Portfolio. Include descriptive comments, strengths, weaknesses, needs, goals.

Conference Records—Use some sort of record for each student on which you note observations and goals that result from portfolio conferences.

Portfolio Evaluation Record—Such a record contains the criteria for overall portfolio evaluation and a way to indicate how the student's Writing Portfolio relates to those criteria.

Class Portfolio Evaluation Record—Some teachers like to gather evaluation information for the class on one chart or record so they can identify group strengths, weaknesses and instructional needs.

Checklist of Writing Skills—This serves as a way to keep track of what writing techniques or skills have been worked on or mastered and which need instructional intervention.

See examples of forms beginning on page 148.

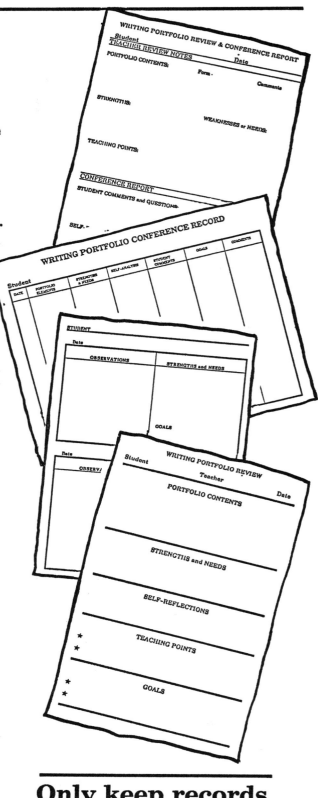

Only keep records you really need.

PORTFOLIOS AND WRITING INSTRUCTION

- What are students learning about writing?
- How is their writing changing?
- How are the writers changing?
- How are students seeing themselves as writers?
- What are they doing well?
- What is giving them trouble?
- What classroom writing instruction is working?
- What isn't working?
- What do they need?

Your writing instruction may never be the same again.

Your students' Writing Portfolios give answers to these questions and others about your writing instruction. There's no delay in the feedback—you get it immediately and repeatedly. This allows you to be constantly adapting the assistance you give students. Your writing instruction can be tailor-made to the writers' needs and intricately tied to the ongoing portfolio and assessment processes.

I finally feel as if I'm really helping kids to be better writers.

A NATURAL PARTNERSHIP

Writing Portfolios and writing instruction are partners in the classroom—they are truly inseparable. It's a good idea to be constantly appraising how they fit together and what each half of this partnership teaches you about the other. For instance:

- The portfolios may reveal that many of your students repeatedly use long and run-on sentences. This prompts a mini-lesson on varying sentence length and structure.

- Or, recent classroom instruction in persuasive writing techniques may cause students to notice how little variety of writing forms their Writing Portfolios have so far this year. They may decide to include an effective persuasive piece among the next selections.

Writing instruction changes forever with the use of Writing Portfolios. Teachers report that they've never gotten such a complete look at student thinking and writing as they do when they review and discuss Writing Portfolios. They become genuinely excited about teaching kids to write. And for many, it is the first time they feel really effective as teachers of writing.

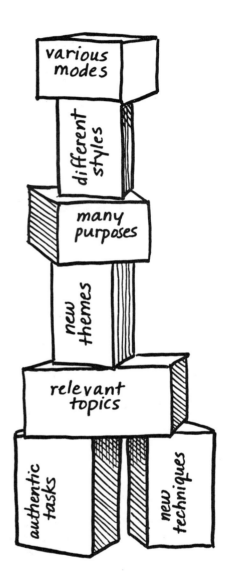

Only give writing assignments that approximate real-life writing tasks.

The best way to take advantage of this partnership for better writing instruction is to keep doing these three things all year long:

1) Keep teaching writing.
2) Listen to what the students and their portfolios are teaching you.
3) Adapt instruction to meet the needs that show up in the portfolio process.

EXPAND WRITING INSTRUCTION

To keep writing flowing throughout the year, continue giving students time and opportunities to write. Constantly expose writers to new styles, forms, ideas and possibilities. Expand the topics for writing and the kinds of writing. Introduce different modes of writing, especially to students in middle and upper grades: expository, narrative, persuasive, descriptive. Introduce new writing skills and techniques also, as you feel your students are ready to try them out.

In all cases where writing is assigned, aim to design assignments that are relevant and interesting to individual writers. Assignments also should be authentic—that is, they should be as much like real-life writing tasks as possible.

The writing process combined with the portfolio process just seems to form a regenerative cycle. As writers extend and expand into different kinds of writing tasks and challenges, their writing grows and develops. New strengths become evident and needs surface, setting the stage for more writing instruction and more celebration of accomplishments. This, in turn, builds writers' confidence and generates more writing.

LEARN FROM THE PORTFOLIOS

Invite your students to join with you in actively figuring out what Writing Portfolios have taught you. Make a list of what has happened in your classroom, what you have learned and what has changed. There is something very rewarding and growth-producing about actually seeing the learning successes and needs in print. Make a chart together and keep it visible as a cause for celebration and a challenge to improve writing. Do this over every few months or every time Writing Portfolios are updated. Then the real excitement begins, because learners can see tangible evidence of their growth.

NEEDS IMPROVEMENT

- more variety in kinds of writing
- more practice in self-reflection
- variety of sentence structure
- organizing ideas
- using examples to support ideas
- descriptive writing
- revisions

DOING WELL

- writing is more interesting
- we're writing more
- better word choices
- good ideas
- writing comes easier
- writing for a special purpose
- telling what's good about our writing
- pre-writing, collecting ideas

PLAN MINI-LESSONS

Once your observations and discussions with students have defined instructional needs, address these needs with short writing lessons on specific topics or techniques. These mini-lessons may be directed to the class or to small groups, depending upon which students need what. They may take five minutes or 20 minutes. Some of them may grow into full-scale, longer writing lessons when necessary. But a great deal of valuable instruction can be accomplished with compact lessons on one very specific skill.

Here are some possible topics for writing mini-lessons.

SOME MINI-LESSON TOPICS...

- planning a piece of writing
- getting ideas organized
- specific kinds of writing
- specific modes of writing
- replacing weak words with stronger or more interesting words
- writing for a specific audience
- good sequence, sense of storyline
- strong voice
- paragraphs that "work"
- creating lines of poetry
- rearranging, expanding or changing sentences to make them effective
- adding details and examples
- eliminating repetitive ideas/words
- eliminating unnecessary ideas/words
- selecting words to set a mood

- writing to accomplish a purpose
- using a variety of sentences
- strong beginnings
- strong endings
- effective middles
- good titles
- using active words
- use of metaphors, exaggeration, figures of speech, humor, irony
- clarity of ideas
- using dialogue
- varying rhymes and rhythms
- increasing reader appeal
- improving transitions
- varying punctuation
- separating facts from opinions
- adding or eliminating bias

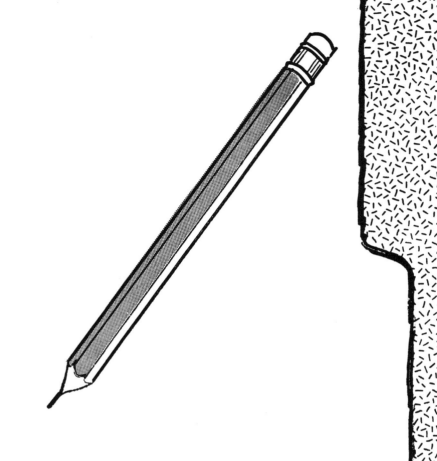

III. EVALUATING
WRITING PORTFOLIOS

GUIDELINES FOR EVALUATION

The real goal of evaluation is to teach students to evaluate themselves.

Throughout the process of developing and using Writing Portfolios, parts or all of the portfolio are examined to analyze what they contain and what they reveal and/or to evaluate for the purpose of judging or finding value. Indeed, analysis and evaluation are intrinsic to the portfolio process.

WHAT? WHO? HOW? WHY?

What evaluation is needed? A Writing Portfolio may be reviewed to learn or make judgments about individual pieces of writing, the whole portfolio or the portfolio process.

Who does it? The student owner, peers, parents, teachers, school officials or anyone else the student chooses can be the evaluator.

How is it done? The forms that a close examination of the portfolio may take are many. Someone looking at it might respond or make judgments orally, on forms, on charts or checklists, through keeping anecdotal notes or records or with a written letter or formal comment.

Why evaluate? Reviewing, analyzing or evaluating the Writing Portfolio can supply students, teachers and others with valuable information about the student's growth and progress. This might be used for personal evaluative information or for academic evaluation. It may also serve to improve classroom instruction, to collect classroom assessment data, to give information for district curriculum decisions or for wide-scale assessment.

How your Writing Portfolios are analyzed and evaluated are up to you. It all depends on the original purposes and goals you set for your portfolio system.

BEFORE YOU EVALUATE

Whenever portfolio elements or whole portfolios are evaluated, by whomever, in whatever form, for whatever purposes, keep these guidelines in mind:

1) You must know what you're after, what you want to find out, before you look closely at the Writing Portfolio for purposes of evaluation.

2) If you are going to make any judgments about what is happening or what is being learned, you must have criteria for evaluation.

3) All criteria must be clear to students.

4) Students should be involved in setting criteria.

5) Evaluation should focus on what the student knows or can do—not on what can't be done.

6) Evaluation is an individual matter. Its purpose is to determine individual progress and growth. Portfolio examination must compare a learner to herself or himself. Portfolios must not be compared to one another. Even when portfolios are compared to a standard, such as a rubric, the emphasis is on growth shown within the portfolio, not in comparison to others.

7) Evaluation never ends. It is ongoing. A learner can always develop, grow, change.

8) Evaluation must involve seeking evidence of progress. Thus, evaluation methods gather information over time. The purpose is not to decide or grade the level where a person is. Evaluation instead must determine where a learner has been, where the learner has come and where the learner is going.

What is being measured? Students should know what constitutes a good performance.

STUDENT SELF-REFLECTION

Self-reflection is stopping to look at yourself as a writer.

One of the most important forms of evaluation that goes on in the portfolio process is student self-evaluation. If a portfolio is to be used in any way to encourage growth or to measure achievement or progress, it must contain some sort of self-evaluation by the student. Most frequently, this analysis or evaluation done by the writer is called **self-reflection.**

WHAT IS SELF-REFLECTION?

Reflection is a time out—the moments a student takes to stop and look at herself or himself as a writer. It is the act of revisiting and reviewing the portfolio to ponder the writing for the purpose of noticing strengths and weaknesses, spotting changes, celebrating growth and finding areas that need improvement.

Often the word **metacognition** is used to describe or accompany the reflecting process. Metacognition is "thinking about thinking." This is really what writers are doing when they review and reflect on their writing. They are asking questions about their thinking and learning processes:

Why do I think this is my best work?

How did I go about creating this?

What was I thinking as I did this?

What was the process I used to do this?

Did I have any problems writing this?

How did I solve problems?

What did I learn from creating this?

What changes do I need to make in my thinking or my process?

WHAT HAPPENS WHEN STUDENTS REFLECT

Self-reflection is, by far, the single most valuable step in the portfolio journey. When they become actively involved in the evaluation of their work, students and teachers find out things they could never discover otherwise about their learning. Some of the good outcomes of the self-reflection process are these:

- Students increase ownership of their learning.

- Students and teachers see how the writers go about creating a piece of writing.

- Teachers learn how the students see their own writing and how they see themselves as writers.

- Students and teachers see how students are using the writing process.

- Teachers learn what students are learning.

- Teachers learn what students think they've done well or haven't done well.

- Students improve in setting writing goals.

- Students increase awareness and understanding of the processes they use for learning.

- Teachers find out about student values, goals, interests, preferences and attitudes.

- There is a shift away from student dependence on the teacher to tell them what's good or right.

- Teachers get a look at the problems students have and how they go about solving them.

- It becomes clear what's working and what's not working in writing instruction.

- Reflection gives direction and shapes purposes for the Writing Portfolios.

Self-reflection is by far the most growth-producing piece of the portfolio process.

CONDITIONS FOR SELF-REFLECTION

Self-reflection doesn't just happen. Like the process of writing, the analyzing of one's work is itself a process to be learned and practiced. It flourishes with instruction, modeling and the right nurturing conditions. For students to engage in any stage or level of reflection, certain conditions must exist and experiences must be underway that will foster its growth.

Classroom Climate—Self-evaluation will flourish in an environment where students' individual differences and developmental levels are honored, their opinions and evaluations are not only allowed but valued, adults are flexible and able to handle disagreement, risks can be taken, independence from the teacher is encouraged, positive feedback is modeled and choice is fostered. The climate must give the message to the student:

"People here care about what you think."

Student Feelings—Students' ability to evaluate their own work will also depend upon emotional conditions such as: how comfortable they feel in the setting, how confident they are with saying their opinions, to what extent they feel their self-evaluations are desired and important, what kinds of feedback they've received when their opinions have been expressed, how dependent they are upon the teacher's approval or evaluation and how able they are to trust their teacher and their peers to hear them and respond with care.

Training in the Writing Process—If students are to reflect on their writing and on the processes they use for writing and learning, it is essential that they be familiar with writing as a process. As they gain more experience with the writing process, writers will be able to engage in more complex, more meaningful and more growth-producing self-evaluations of their learning.

Experience with Metacognition—Metacognition is "thinking about thinking." Students must use metacognition in order to analyze their writing, examine the processes they use, to solve problems with their writing or to consider future writing goals. Thus learning to think about the ways they think and learn provides a sound base for self-evaluation of their writing and their portfolios.

Opportunities for Dialogue—The classroom in which students reflect upon writing must be one filled with experiences and activities that help reflection become fluent. Discussion and dialogue among classroom members is crucial for this. Some things that teach and nurture reflection are student-teacher conferences and discussions, peer response groups, sharing of work among writers, reflecting on others' work and listening to and giving constructive feedback.

Time—Good self-reflection will not happen without time. Students need regular sessions of sufficient length for considering their work in order to make some judgments about it. In any classroom, students will learn how important the process of self-evaluation is partly by seeing how much time the class schedule allows for reflection on their writing and their portfolios.

WAYS TO REFLECT

The forms that self-reflections take are as varied as the classrooms and students using portfolios. There are many different effective and workable ways for writers to analyze, evaluate or comment on their work. Some possibilities are:

- open-ended sentences to finish
- questions for writers to respond to
- comments written on sticky notes or index cards and attached to the writing
- evaluative essays
- brief comments or sentences
- metacognitive letters
- checklists to complete
- commercially-designed response forms
- teacher or student-designed reflection forms

This writing was hard for me because ....

Reflections may be written or oral. They may be saved on paper, cards, drawings, audiotapes or videotapes. In many portfolio classrooms, teachers and students try a variety of approaches to self, peer, parent or teacher reflections. They test different ways and experiment with different forms until they find the ones that work for them.

I chose this as my best writing because it started with a bang and kept right on popping,...

Dear Mrs. Foster, I have compared my most exciting and my most dull pieces of writing. I hope you will notice how.........

This is a strong argument because........

TYPES OF REFLECTIONS

Self-reflections are of many different types, depending on students' experience, metacognition and self-evaluation. Reflections may focus on:

- why a piece was selected
- attributes of a particular piece
- comparisons of two or more pieces of work
- what a piece shows about the writer
- evaluation of the whole portfolio
- analysis of the writer's process
- analysis of the portfolio process

Reflections may address:

- **Writing appearance and conventions**—length of the piece, number of topics, paragraphing, handwriting, neatness, space between letters and sentences, illustrations, punctuation, capitalization, spelling, sentence length

- **Ideas and content**—creativity, originality, number of ideas included, interest or appeal of content, word choice, details and facts included

- **Writing forms and techniques**—beginnings, endings, phrasing, variety of sentences, dialogue, titles, sequencing, transitions, use of different forms, fitting form to purpose or audience

- **Processes**—use of writing process, how writer goes about creating or problem-solving, ways the writer works or thinks, effort, attitudes

- **Growth**—how writing or portfolio shows progress, change and/or the writer's development

Self-reflection invites students to be a part of their own assessment.

I really improved on adding details to my writing....

HOW STUDENTS GROW AT SELF-REFLECTION

become more comfortable evaluating their work

↓

number of comments increases

↓

comment on more aspects of writing

↓

look at themselves as writers

↓

notice and appreciate change

↓

start to compare works

↓

move from emphasis on one piece to focus on what all the work shows

↓

grow in ability to assess their own achievement and progress

GROWTH OF REFLECTION

You can expect students' reflections to grow and change with time. Usually, writers begin with simple, short reflections that focus on individual pieces of writing, relate obvious aspects of the writing (such as neatness, length, spelling) or that make brief comments about why something was selected for the portfolio. As they gain experience with reflecting, students will increase the number and length of evaluative comments, improve their clarity of expression, discuss more elements of their writing and their portfolios, move toward more complex evaluations and greater use of metacognitive processes and become more comfortable with writing and with reflecting.

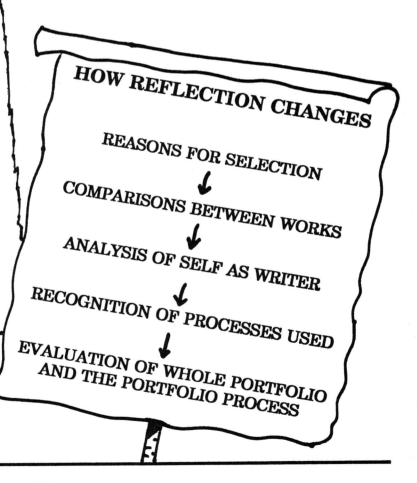

HOW REFLECTION CHANGES

REASONS FOR SELECTION

↓

COMPARISONS BETWEEN WORKS

↓

ANALYSIS OF SELF AS WRITER

↓

RECOGNITION OF PROCESSES USED

↓

EVALUATION OF WHOLE PORTFOLIO AND THE PORTFOLIO PROCESS

REFLECTION: AN ONGOING PROCESS

When the term "self-reflection" is used in connection with portfolios, it's common to envision a written analysis of a work or of the portfolio. Yes, that is self-reflection. But it is only one example—one important piece in the large puzzle. Reflection is far broader than a written evaluation on a card or piece of paper. Students evaluate and reflect in many ways as they work on every aspect of the portfolio process—not just when they are responding to a piece selected for the Writing Portfolio. They also reflect as they:

- make decisions about topics for writing
- generate and organize ideas for writing
- revise and polish writing
- collect and save work samples
- sort and organize portfolios
- make choices about what to include or exclude
- share writing with peers and parents
- respond to each other's writing
- interview peers or work in editing groups
- prepare for and hold portfolio conferences
- set future writing goals

Help students recognize all the reflective activities they are involved in. Constant discussion during these experiences will serve to strengthen their abilities to do good self-evaluation.

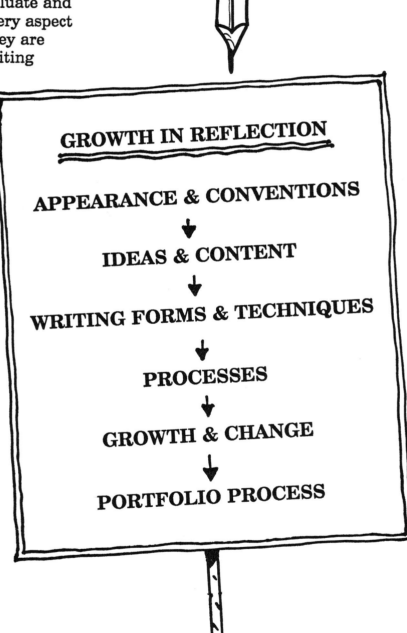

GROWTH IN REFLECTION

APPEARANCE & CONVENTIONS
↓
IDEAS & CONTENT
↓
WRITING FORMS & TECHNIQUES
↓
PROCESSES
↓
GROWTH & CHANGE
↓
PORTFOLIO PROCESS

Students must be taught how to self-reflect.

If I could do yesterday's lesson over I'd read you more examples of good description

This week my goal is to finish my photo essay and share it with you

I think this worked well because we read tons of news articles before writing our own

TEACHING STUDENTS TO SELF-REFLECT

When you think about asking students to reflect on their writing, be aware that most of them have never been asked to do this before. They'll need to be taught how to do it. The most important way they learn this is by seeing the teacher model reflection. They also learn by trying and practicing evaluative techniques on their own and other's writing. Teaching of reflection can start with simple activities and increase in complexity throughout the year, growing to include a greater variety of techniques and approaches.

What follows are suggested steps for teaching students to reflect on writing.

1) **Model reflective approaches in the classroom.**

   Start by paying attention to your language, attitudes and messages. Infuse your teaching and discussions with students with such evaluative statements as:

   Here's what I noticed about this lesson...

   I learned.......from the poems you wrote...

   I thought this worked better than what we did yesterday because...

   I'd like us to start over on......because...

   Something surprising in your work was...

   One of my goals for this week is...

   I chose to do this today because...

   I had a hard time with this lesson because...

   I had fun with this activity because...

   It seems that this is the way you approached this process: you started with......and went on to...

2) Practice reflective activities in the classroom.

"Do" reflection frequently in connection with many activities and subject areas, such as:

- Ask students to place in a paper lunch bag five items that are important to them or tell something about who they are and explain to a small group why each was chosen.

- At the end of each school day, ask students to choose the high point of the day and the low point of the day, and tell why for each choice.

- After any activity, reflect on what the class liked about it, what the class did well, what they had trouble with, what they learned about themselves from it, what they'd like to do differently or learn next time.

- After any lesson or activity, have individuals meet with a peer and tell:

  What I did best...

  What I liked and didn't like...

  How I went about doing this...

  What I learned from this...

  What I'd do differently next time...

- Ask questions that get students reflecting on classroom experiences or work they're doing:

  How did this compare to the activity we did yesterday?

  What was important about what we did?

  What needs more work? Why?

  What was your favorite thing to do? Why?

  Did you have problems with anything?

  Do we need to work more on this activity?

This is important because it's about my dad and he thinks I'm great!

The best part about Julie's letter is the shocking ending.

THIS IS MY BEST BECAUSE I REALLY WORKED HARD ON IT.

this is good because I wrote a whole page.

I started by writing down 40 good spooky words, then I grouped them into phrases.

Students are no longer dependent on the teacher to decide what is good or right.

3) **Do lots of oral reflections on writing.**

Once students have watched the teacher model reflective behaviors and have themselves practiced reflective attitudes and questions, they will be ready to begin oral reflections on writing. They can respond to writing samples you read to them or provide for them, or to samples done by themselves or peers. Oral reflections may be done with the whole class, in small groups or through peer interviews. Help students ask and answer questions such as those below. (See also the statements and questions on pages 130–133.)

What is strong about this piece of writing?

What would you change in this writing?

What kinds of reactions do others have to this?

What was the best thing the writer did?

Did you have any problems as you wrote this?

How do you feel about this piece of writing?

What would you look for if you were evaluating this piece of writing?

How did you go about creating this?

What do you think was important to the author of this piece?

Is there a piece of writing you'd like to work on more? What would you do to it?

Which writing would you like to throw away? Why?

Which writing is your most important? Why?

Which writing was the hardest for you? Why?

Which piece was the most enjoyable? Why?

Which piece of writing is your best? Why?

What did you learn from doing this piece?

4) **Make a selection for the Writing Portfolio and write a reflection explaining your choice.**

Agree on a kind of selection that will be made, or allow individuals to decide separately. Ask students to choose a piece for the Writing Portfolio and write the reasons for the selection.

This is my best piece of writing because....

I selected this as my favorite because...

This is my most important piece because...

I'd like to burn this piece because...

I would like to keep working on this because...

This is my hardest writing because...

I felt good about this piece because...

Katy Bridges
4/22/93

How to make Salsa

I chose to Burn this piece of writing because it wasn't very interesting and it is a piece of writing that you would probably put down after the first sentence. It sounds like something that you would get out of a cookbook.. It seems to drag on and on too. Zzzzzzz.

5) **Compare pieces of writing.**

After several selections have been made and reflected upon (as in #4), involve students in discussions that compare pieces of writing. Ask them to think about such questions as:

What kind of writing does each piece represent?

How are some different pieces alike in the writing?

What are the strengths of different pieces?

How do the weaknesses compare?

What writing techniques are the same or different?

How have others responded to different pieces?

After oral reflections, students can sort through their Writing Portfolios and select two pieces for a written reflection that compares and contrasts the two pieces.

"I want this in my portfolio because it's the longest writing I've ever done. It's a whole sentence."
- Jeremy, age 6 -

Comparison

"The Awful Mistake" is much much better then "Late One Night" because I've learned so much about writing. "Mistake" has more detail and more strong words that really describe my feeling about the mistake. There's so much more of me in it. In "One Night" lots of ideas were out of order and sort of creek. Nobody was very impressed with it. All the sentences were too long. "Mistake" has sentences of different kinds and lengths. It is a much cooler piece of writing. HURRAY o I'VE IMPROVED!

6) Help students reflect on themselves as writers.

This may be done by examining individual pieces and through reviewing and considering the portfolios as a whole. Dedicate plenty of time for students to examine and discuss how they handle the writing process, what their works show about them as writers and how they've grown or changed. Whether they do this orally or in writing, alone, in groups, with peers or with teachers, encourage them to ask such questions as:

What does this piece show about you as a writer?

What would someone learn about you as a writer from looking at your Writing Portfolio?

How has your writing changed or grown?

How do you handle the writing process? What parts of the process are you good at?..not good at?

What kind of process did you follow as you wrote this piece?

What are your strengths as a writer?

What kinds of problems do you face as a writer?

How do you deal with problems in your writing?

What improvements have you noticed over time?

What forms of writing are most comfortable for you?

Which forms are most uncomfortable?

What are your goals for yourself as a writer?

After students have had opportunities to reflect upon a collection of their work by answering questions such as these, give them time to do a written reflection for their portfolios in which they tell what they know about writing, how they've grown or changed as a writer or what the portfolio shows about them as a writer.

> **It is through self-evaluation that students begin to see themselves as REAL writers.**

The 8 pieces of writing in my portfolio show my growth as a writer.

In the beginning I wrote pretty boring sentences with no details or sparkly words.

My recent stuff has many details to make things exciting. I use more outrageous words now. My ideas are also much better organized .....

> To whoever reads my portfolio,
>
> I hope you will notis that I wrote many different kinds of writing. My Portfolio shows that I am a good Worker and that I improved at getting things in the rite order. You shuold see how funny I am from the silly poem and the flying Banana story. I hope...

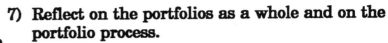

7) Reflect on the portfolios as a whole and on the portfolio process.

At some point, students of all ages should have the experience of reflecting on their Writing Portfolios as a whole. This is a time for them to revisit and examine portfolios. They can make decisions about how to organize the portfolio and about what to remove or keep.

You might plan for this once or twice a year, or it might happen naturally each time students prepare the portfolios for review by someone else or get ready for a portfolio conference. Written reflections may address not only what the writer has learned about his or her growth as a writer, but also what the writer's thoughts are about the portfolio process. Often such an overall analysis can be done in the form of a metacognitive letter to the teacher or anyone else who looks at the portfolio. Students can reflect on and explain:

What's in this portfolio and why

How I organized this portfolio and why

What I think this portfolio tells about me

What I hope a reader learns from my portfolio

What I learned from the portfolio process

What I think about the portfolio process (strengths, weaknesses, etc.)

What changes should be made in our portfolio use

Reflection uncovers truths about the writing that even the writer didn't know.

SOME REMINDERS ABOUT REFLECTION

As you approach the task of helping writers learn and grow in self-evaluation, keep in mind:

Reflection must be taught. Most students have never been asked to analyze or evaluate their work, especially in a formal or written way. Don't assume that you can tell them what reflection is and that they'll be able to do it. Many are so dependent on teacher evaluation that they'll resist making their own decisions about what is good. They need plenty of time, modeling, practice, guidance—and especially permission in order to learn and feel comfortable with self–reflection.

Reflect soon after writing. Writers should pause to think about a work as soon as possible after it has been completed. In many cases, a writer reflects automatically before a piece is finished. The sooner a writer reflects, the fresher will be the insights, the clearer the processes, the stronger the awareness of successes and problems.

Students will grow at different rates. No two writers will make progress in self-evaluation on the same time schedule. Allow them to grow at individual rates.

Celebrate the stage of reflection—whatever it is. Reinforce each student's self-evaluations, no matter how simple they may seem. Do not be discouraged by short statements or reflections of little content. The stage where a writer is now is the foundation on which growth is built.

Reflection knows no subject-area boundaries. When students learn to evaluate their writing and themselves as writers, these skills and attitudes will spill over into all subject areas.

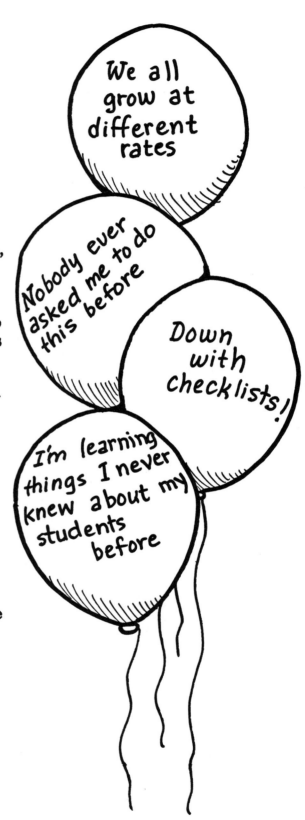

Reflect—
the sooner the
better

Every stage
of reflection
deserves
celebration

So—
CELEBRATE
!

Don't abandon any of the stages. Although writers gradually move toward more complex reflections, the tasks that seem simpler are still valuable. No writer gets too advanced as to be beyond the need for scrutinizing pieces and analyzing all aspects of their writing. This is what helps writing improve.

Beware of forms that are restrictive. Ready-made forms and checklists may be helpful when you're getting started with reflections. But forms that are too narrow or rigid tend to limit student reflections. And filling out a checklist can seem like just another assignment. Open-ended reflections allow the most freedom for writers to really analyze their work. If you do use forms, the best ones are those that you and your students develop.

Let young writers dictate reflections. Students needn't be able to write in order to learn to reflect on their creations or compositions. Very young writers can dictate their works and reflections to an adult, older student or a tape recorder. As soon as young students are able to write, do give them chances to write their own reflections, even if the spelling and writing are almost unintelligible. This makes them feel like real writers. It also generates more honest reflections.

Students often find it hard to "brag" about themselves. Don't be surprised to find that your writers are reluctant to write or say congratulatory or positive things about their writing. It's hard for many of us to say, "I'm good at this" in public. Some students will need plenty of gentle encouragement before they feel comfortable with this. The habit of celebrating writing strengths as a group will go a long way toward creating the freedom students need to openly feel good about their accomplishments.

FOSTERING SELF-REFLECTION

Writers of all ages will grow in ability to evaluate their own work and progress when they are provided with good examples and direction. One of the best ways the teacher can do this is through asking questions and modeling language that fosters reflection. So when you are deciding on questions for interviews, peer response groups, conferences or reflection forms, make sure you think of those which:

- ask for close examination of a piece of writing
- encourage comparisons of works
- get students thinking about how they function as writers
- encourage use of metacognition
- require analysis of writing skills used
- request analysis of the processes used
- promote consideration of affective areas such as confidence, interest, effort and enjoyment
- alert students to look for change and growth
- encourage evaluation of the whole portfolio

The best thing about keeping a portfolio is....

The worst thing about keeping a portfolio is....

This is my best

I struggled with.......

What I need to improve is....

I need help with....

I chose this because.....

What I like about it is.......

Here's how I have grown....

Something in my portfolio that surprised me was....

I'm getting better at....

This is   use....

On my next piece, I'd like to work on..........

This piece shows my writing strengths are.......

If I wanted to work more on this I would....

As I wrote this, I worked hard on........

This is one of my best pieces because.....

This was hard because...

Something that has a good beginning.............

This was fun to write because..............

What I learned from doing writing is....

I'd like to throw this writing away because....

The difference between my present work and my goal is....

What I need to do to reach my goal is...

What I notice that's better about my writing is.....

Something I want to finish is .....

I'd like everybody to see this.......because....

When I start writing something, I feel....

When I finish writing something, I feel...

By looking at this portfolio you can tell....

The best thing about writing is....

The worst thing about writing is....

If I could change this, I would....

What I've learned about writing essays is....

What was important to me when I wrote this was..

My Writing Portfolio is....

By looking at my portfolio you can tell....

QUESTIONS THAT PROMOTE SELF-REFLECTION

Why did you select this piece?

What makes this your best (favorite, most satisfying, hardest, least favorite) piece?

How did you go about writing this?

Can you describe the process you used?

What do you see as the special strengths of this piece?

What did you struggle with or what problems did you run into? How did you solve them?

What goals did you set for yourself before you wrote this? How did you accomplish them?

If you could work on this further, what would you do?

How does this piece compare with your other writing?

Does this show improvement over other pieces?

How would you like to have this piece evaluated?

What reactions did you get from others on this writing?

What would you like to write about next?

What forms of writing would you like to try?

What makes a good writer?

Are you a good writer? Why?

How would you describe your progress as a writer?

When you write something, what process do you usually use?

Where do you need help as a writer?

What does the teacher do that helps you?

How do others' reflections help you?

MORE QUESTIONS THAT PROMOTE SELF-REFLECTION

What have you learned about writing?

What do you need to learn about writing?

What do you usually like to write about?

What writing forms are most comfortable for you? Why?

What writing forms are least comfortable for you? Why?

What writing forms would you like to try or improve?

What part of the writing process goes well for you?

What part of the writing process gives you trouble?

How has your writing changed since the year began?

What goals do you have for yourself as a writer?

Of all the writing in your portfolio, which do you feel most confident about? Why?

Has your confidence about writing changed since the beginning of the year? How?

What do you most enjoy about writing?

What do you least enjoy about writing?

How do you decide what to put in your Writing Portfolio?

How have you organized your Writing Portfolio? Why?

What does your portfolio show about you as a writer?

Does your portfolio show any changes in your writing? How?

What will others learn from your portfolio?

What have you learned from doing a portfolio?

What would you change about the portfolio process?

My Best because...
I wod like a panda
jst like the won I rote
about it wus a good
ideea.

Name Brad

My writing is better now. My handwriting
is neater and my writing has many
intresting topics not just all stories ecther
but puems, news articals, conversations,
ads, and songs. I'm awsum at writing
songs. I think I could be a song writer
when I grow up. Maybe I'll try some
of those sad country songs. I need to
stop making everything so long. I have
a bad habit of going on and on and on

**SAMPLE
STUDENT
REFLECTIONS**

PURSUASIVE LETTER

SARA
11-27-93

A SKATING RINK IN ASHLAND

I CHOSE THIS AS "MY MOST IMPORTANT"
PIECE OF WRITING BECAUSE IF I SENT
A COPY OF THIS TO THE MAYOR, THE CHAMBER
OF COMMERCE, OR THE FAIR BOARD IT COULD
BE HELP CONVINCE PEOPLE TO BUILD A RINK
IN SOUTHERN OREGON. (ASHLAND & MEDFORD) AND
THAT IS REALLY IMPORTANT TO ME.

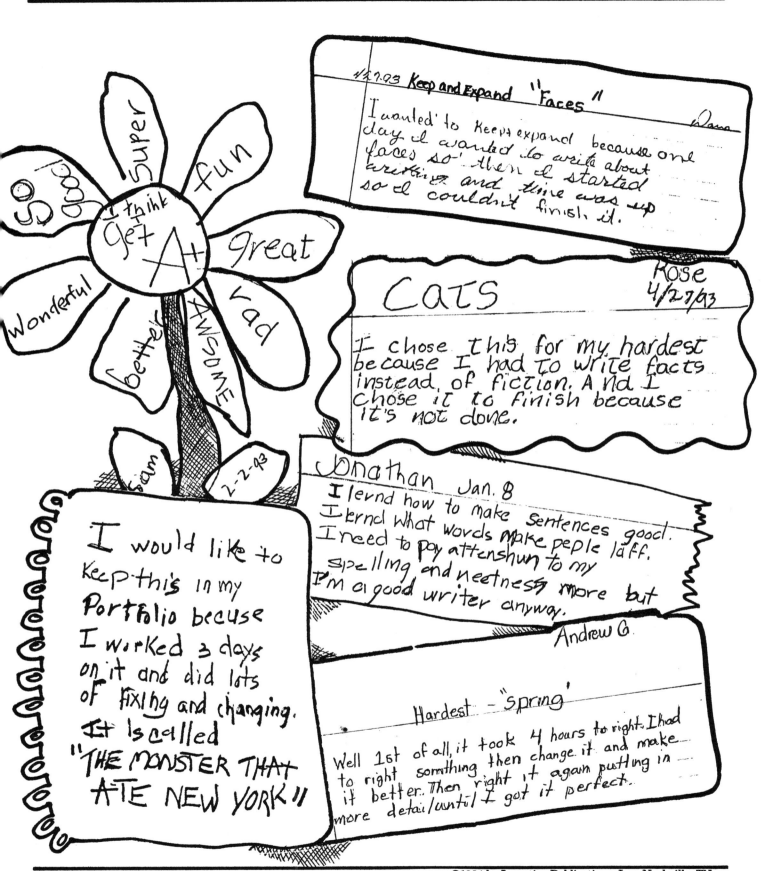

4/27/93 Keep and Expand "Faces"

Dana

I wanted to keep expand because one day I wanted to write about faces so then I started writing and time was up so I couldn't finish it.

Rose
4/27/93

CATS

I chose this for my hardest because I had to write facts instead of fiction. And I chose it to finish because it's not done.

Jonathan   Jan. 8

I lernd how to make sentences good. I lernd what words make peple laff. I need to pay attenshun to my spelling and neetness more but I'm a good writer anyway.

I would like to keep this in my Portfolio becuse I worked 3 days on it and did lots of fixing and changing. It is called "THE MONSTER THAT ATE NEW YORK"

Andrew G.

Hardest - "spring"

Well 1st of all, it took 4 hours to right. I had to right something then change it and make it better. Then right it again putting in more detail/until I got it perfect.

So good Super fun
great
Wonderful   rad
better   Awsome
I think get A+
Sam   2-2-93

The Eyes Have It!

Eyes are so clever and keen
They see what you are and where you've been
Just when you think you're out of sight
Some eyes appear out of the night
Eyes watch your movements for a while
Then they surprise you with a smile
Don't worry about the fact that you've been seen
These eyes are mine - and they're friendly . . . . they're not mean.

Shelly A.
3-7-93

I wrote EYES to let people know that you don't always have to be afraid of somebody looking at you or watching you. Actually, I think I wrote it to help me feel that some eyes are not watching to spy on you or make you feel bad. I learned that writing lets out your feelings. Also this piece has some good rhyme.

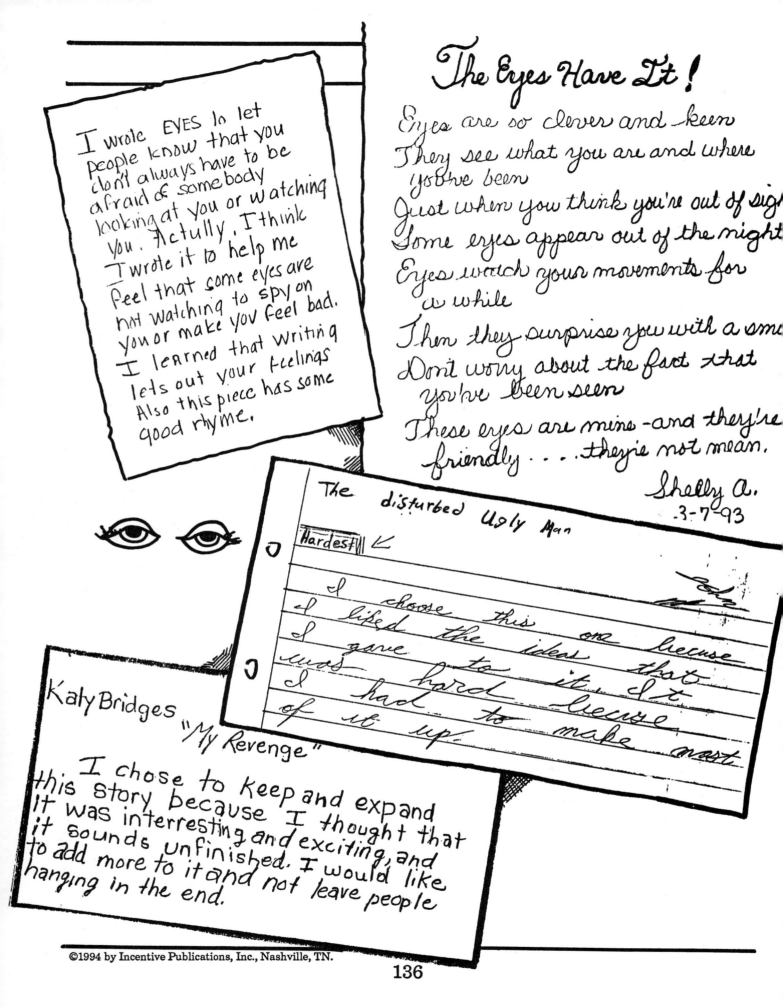

The disturbed Ugly Man

Hardest

I chose this one
I liked the idea becuse
I gave to it, It
was hard becuse
I had to make
of it up. most

Katy Bridges "My Revenge"

I chose to keep and expand this story because I thought that it was interresting and exciting, and it sounds unfinished. I would like to add more to it and not leave people hanging in the end.

ODE TO MY GYM SHOES

If you only knew
How I felt about you.......

You look pretty beat up,
My old friends.
You've been stomped on
And tromped on,
Dragged through mud,
Pounded into hard pavement,
Kicked against balls and killer walls,
You've been crammed into a gym bag
And forced to survive in the dark,
        smelly locker room.
You even grew some digusting slimy mold
        when I never let you dry out.
You've carried my sweaty feet
        through miles of p.e. torture.
You've cushioned my tired body.
You've never complained, though you're
        all dirty and torn.
You never seemed to mind how hard you
        were worn.

If only you knew
How I felt about you......
You were awesome when you were new
I was so proud of you
But now that you're used and abused,
You're really my favorite shoes.

Tracy Smith 2-10-93

SAMPLE
STUDENT REFLECTIONS

I chose my poem about my gym shoes as the piece of writing that surprised me. I didn't know it could be so fun to write like a letter to something not alive like these old shoes. It was fun to think about them as a friend. It surprised me to go back and read this and see how it made me smile to read it. I did a pretty good job of using personification I think. I used some good words, too like killer walls, crammed, stomped, tromped, abused. The peers who read this said they liked the rhyme at the beginning and end. I think that was pretty clever and affective writing. If I could work on it more I would try to think of a different ending. The rhyme isn't so hot and the end is the weakest part.

I tryed very hard
This shows that I
can write hole storys.
I can write sooooooo good.

Tammy S.
4-1-92

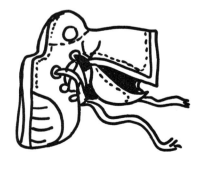

REFLECTIONS FROM OTHERS

Writers of all ages and at all stages of development can benefit greatly from having others respond to individual pieces of writing or to the whole Writing Portfolio. Teachers, peers, parents, friends and others can offer feedback that is both supportive and constructive for the writers.

In all cases, when others respond to students' portfolios, they must be taught beforehand that helpful responses are:

- non-judgmental
- supportive and affirming
- specific—identifying a particular trait or strength

PEER REFLECTIONS

Most of the suggestions, forms, questions and phrases suggested on pages 114–137 as possibilities for self-reflection can be used for peers to respond to one another. Students learn to respond to others' writing right along with learning to self-evaluate. When they prepare reflections for peers, not only do they learn about another student as a person and writer, but they also see things that help them improve their own writing.

Try several ways to have peers reflect on writing: peer editing or evaluating groups, peer oral interviews, peer conferences, peer written responses.

When peers respond to others' writing, they learn about their own.

PARENT RESPONSES

When parents are invited to take part in portfolio evaluation, they learn about what their children are learning. They also are given a way to support and affirm their child's growth when they see themselves as a valued and important part of the assessment process. Parent responses to portfolios can also be gained through many of the methods outlined for self–reflection. Specific times when parents might be asked to reflect on portfolios are:

- Parent Night or Open House
- student–led parent portfolio conferences
- Writing Portfolio parties
- portfolio take–home night (portfolio accompanied by Parent Portfolio Survey Form)

RESPONSES FROM OTHERS

Teachers can respond to the Writing Portfolio in any of the ways already mentioned. Often, teachers attach notes to pieces of writing or respond orally during conferences. Students may also invite reflections from anyone they wish: friends, neighbors, students in other classes, the principal.

PARENT RESPONSE TO WRITING PORTFOLIO

Dear Parent(s)...

Thank you for joining in on the sharing of my Writing Portfolio. Please write your thoughts about the portfolio.

What was your favorite part of the portfolio? I loved the cartoon about your science project on worms. It taught me all about worms and it was also very funny. I liked the "wormy" words you used too!

Did anything in the portfolio surprise you? Yes! all the writing you've done—the amount. You've written so much different stuff—and it's so good.

What did you learn about my writing from the portfolio? I see that you've grown in expressing your ideas and writing more kinds of writing forms. It also looks like you've learned many new words.

Compliments and comments:
- portfolio looks cool
- Table of Contents really helped me
- illustrations are wonderful
- you're a good poet.

Jamie's Mom
Signature

Portfolios invite parent praise for learners.

ANALYZING PIECES OF WRITING

Ongoing, informal evaluation of writing is every bit as valuable as scoring writing on a writing scale.

Individual pieces of writing may be analyzed informally by the student, the teacher, peers, parents or others. Or it can be evaluated formally to gain a score or grade. Whatever methods are used for evaluating individual pieces of writing, one rule is crucial to follow:

Whenever a piece is analyzed individually—even if it is scored with a scoring model—it must be re-evaluated or re-examined later as a part of the whole Writing Portfolio.

INFORMAL EVALUATION OF WRITING

Students are constantly evaluating their writing as they review portfolios, revise writing, make selections, prepare portfolios for review and prepare for conferences. Much evaluative information on individual works of writing is made available to the writer and the teacher informally through self-reflection, teacher, peer and parent reflections, portfolio conferences, class discussions, peer interviews, teacher anecdotal notes.

Such evaluation, though labeled "informal," is every bit as valuable as the "formal" scoring of works. In fact, most of the information gained about a student's work and progress is gained through these ongoing, informal means.

FORMAL EVALUATION OF WRITING

For more formal evaluation leading to a score, writing samples can be analyzed with a scoring guide or rubric. These are designed to evaluate writing performance by measuring specific traits or characteristics of the writing such as ideas, word choice, voice, organization, sentence structure and conventions. A scoring guide includes a rating scale and criteria for judging writing.

Self-reflections

PORTFOLIO REVIEWS

RESPONSE FROM NEIGHBORS

Peer reflections

parent Conferences

SCORED WRITING SAMPLES

Teacher Reflections

PORTFOLIOS

CONFERENCE NOTES

group sharing

Peer Interviews

Some states and school districts have their own scoring models which teachers and students use to score writing. It is often very useful to create your own rubric to truly examine the writing skills and processes being taught in your classroom. It is also very beneficial **for students to be involved in creating the scoring guide or rubric.** To create your own rubric:

1) Identify the goals or traits you want to rate.
2) Create a rating score and define each number.
3) Write the criteria for each trait at each score level using specific characteristics that will be used to judge the writing.

Such scoring guides are useful for **occasional** analysis of writing samples. It is neither necessary nor desirable to score every piece of writing.

IDEAS....5 ORGANIZATION...4
WORD CHOICE....3 SENTENCES...4
VOICE....4 CONVENTIONS....5

The Eyes Have It!

Eyes are so clever and keen
They see what you are and what you've been
Just when you think you're out of sight
Some eyes appear out of the night
Eyes watch your movements for a while
Then they surprise you with a smile
Don't worry about the fact that you've been seen
These eyes are mine — and they're friendly ... they're not mean.
Shelly A.
3-7-93

SAMPLE RUBRIC

	IDEAS	Word Choice	Voice	Organization	Sentence Structure	Conventions
1	lacks clear main idea, purpose unclear, no supporting details, makes no point	reader gets no picture, repetitive words, dull or overused words, no new words tried	dull and lifeless, reader gets no sense of who writer is, no passion about the topic	sentence and idea arrangements confusing, ideas disconnected, no paragraphing, no clear beginning or end, hard to follow	confusing, incomplete or run-on sentences, no variety, sentence structure makes it hard to read and understand	many errors in spelling, usage, punctuation, paragraphing, difficult to follow
2	main idea somewhat developed, wanders from idea some, few details, purpose not real clear, partially makes a point	some word variety, uses adequate but ordinary words, few fresh or exciting words	writer shows some of self, involvement is inconsistent, only minor sense of who the writer is and what he/she feels or believes	some good sequence and paragraphing but inconsistent, weak beginning or ending, some ideas out of place, somewhat confusing to follow	some variety, some run-on or incomplete, mechanical, not fluid, sometimes hard to understand	noticeable errors that make reading occasionally confusing or difficult
3	clear purpose and main idea, makes point well, good supporting details, has control of topic, interesting to read	strong, specific words, interesting and colorful, variety of words, tried new and unusual words, words paint a picture for reader	fully involved, true interest and excitement, individual style and personality show through, enthusiastic, reader gets a real feel for the author	good, clear sequence, effective paragraphs, details lead to main point, strong beginning and conclusion, writing makes sense	variety of kinds, correct structure, sentences make meaning clear	few errors, proofreading evident, very readable and easy to understand

ANALYZING THE WHOLE PORTFOLIO

When you set out to evaluate the portfolio as a whole, what you're really doing is trying to build as complete as possible a picture of the writer's achievement, abilities, attitudes, strengths, needs and progress over time. Gather enough of the kinds of information to give a clear picture of each student as a person, a learner, a writer.

TOOLS FOR EVALUATION

The ways you devise to gather such information are tools to help find out what is going on with each student's development. Here is a suggested list of the places, tools and methods that can supply you with evaluation information:

- anecdotal notes (ongoing record of observations from daily work—characteristics, problems, needs, strengths)

- notes from teacher portfolio review

- conference records

- students' self-evaluations

- portfolio evaluation record (notes kept at each in-depth portfolio analysis 2-4 times a year or record of portfolio scoring by rubric)

- portfolio scoring guide or rubric

- class profile of portfolio progress/needs (a record from analysis of portfolios to identify group instructional needs and successes)

Don't use more tools than you need, but do gather information in a variety of ways. A scoring guide with a numerical rating is just one way to evaluate the portfolio. If scoring is used, supplement it with plenty of less formal, anecdotal, descriptive information and samples. Each method above paints a part of the total picture of the writer.

Each evaluation technique you use paints another part of the total picture of the writer.

USING A SCORING GUIDE FOR EVALUATION

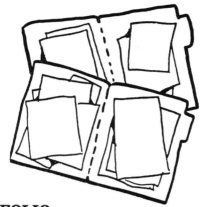

In some classrooms, teachers and students evaluate portfolios with the aid of a scoring guide or rubric. Many districts or even states are providing portfolio scoring guides for classroom, district or state-wide use. These provide descriptions of a portfolio at various levels. It is absolutely necessary that students understand the criteria descriptions in the scoring guide. It is even better when rubrics are created locally by the teachers and students using them. Students benefit greatly when they have a role in setting the criteria for evaluating their Writing Portfolios.

Here is a sample of a scoring rubric for Writing Portfolios:

WRITING PORTFOLIO
Scoring Guide

	1 Needs Much Improvement	2 Adequate	3 Strong
Variety and Quantity of Writing	limited quantity, little or no variety of forms, not a broad collection	acceptable number, variety and versatility of writing forms and purposes	rich variety of kinds of writing showing versatility of writing attempts and ability
Writing Skills and Traits	limited demonstration of various writing techniques, weak development of traits	evidence of experience with several traits, attention to text and surface features, ideas are developed	good control of several writing skills and traits, ideas and organization lead to clear, understandable writing
Writing Process	shows little or no grasp of writing strategies and processes	uses the writing process, can describe how he/she approaches writing	obvious facility with all phases of the writing process, samples of stages are evident in portfolio
Evidence of Growth	little change seen from early to late pieces, little sense of self as writer, little engagement with writing, poor at setting personal goals	some growth seen from early to later pieces, some sense of self as writer, evidence of goal setting	progress evident, increased use of writing processes and skills, identifies self as writer, sets personal standards and goals
Self-Evaluation	no reflections or narrow, one-dimensional evaluations	expanding self-evaluations, able to identify characteristics of own writing	clear, specific reflections increasing in variety and depth
Portfolio Processes	poor presentation and organization, has difficulty with preparing and caretaking portfolio	shows organization, ownership, interest, increased independence in managing own portfolio	takes responsibility, independence in managing portfolio, good appearance and organization
Personal Involvement and Attitude	little or no attachment to portfolio or sense of accomplishment or pride	takes pride in ownership, takes some initiative and control of portfolio, feels sense of worth	takes great pride in ownership, enthusiastic, enjoys taking responsibility for learning

EVALUATING THE PORTFOLIO PROCESS

Your main evaluation goals, of course, have to do with recognizing student growth and achievement. However, don't neglect to take a close look at the process of doing Writing Portfolios. Stop now and then and ask students to give you feedback on what is happening. Ask yourself the same questions you'll ask them—questions such as:

How do you feel about our portfolio process?

What have you learned from doing a portfolio?

What is working well?

What isn't working so well?

Should we change anything in our process?

WHAT TO DO AT THE END OF THE YEAR

The information you gain from all the various approaches to the evaluation of Writing Portfolios will give you valuable insights into each student, provide valuable assessment information, change and improve writing instruction and improve the portfolio process. In addition, the portrait of the student that the portfolio creates can be valuable to the next teacher, to the student in the future or to the school.

For these reasons, the Writing Portfolio, or some samples from it, may be placed into a permanent or ongoing portfolio. This may be passed along to the next grade or even follow the student for several years. Students can create the Pass-Along Portfolio with the desired or required elements (or copies of these elements). Then, most of them will be delighted to take home the "real" Writing Portfolio and keep it forever.

IV. SOME FINAL ADVICE AND SAMPLE FORMS

WORDS OF ADVICE

Some final words of advice as you embark or continue on your adventure with Writing Portfolios:

Make sure you know what you're after. Ask yourself again and again, "Where are we going?" and "How will we know when we get there?" Everything you do is based on the portfolio purposes and goals. So keep these in mind at all times.

Don't bite off more than you can chew. Start small and build as you're comfortable. Keep your system as simple as possible. And take your time—move into it slowly, at your own pace.

Plan carefully. You will never be sorry for time you've spent planning, anticipating hitches, solving management questions, thinking ahead.

Keep your own portfolio. Start right away creating a personal portfolio. Also, build your own Writing Portfolio along with students. Doing it yourself is one of the best ways to learn about portfolios.

Get some company. The portfolio process is new, different and far from simple. You'll have more fun, greater growth and success, and probably much less frustration if you work at this with a partner or several other colleagues.

Be alert for problems. Using portfolios can be messy business. You can be assured that problems and pitfalls will arise. Keep your eyes and ears open for them and tackle them with students and/or colleagues as soon as they arise.

Listen to your students. This cannot be said often enough. Writing Portfolios will have greater benefits if you keep listening to students tell you what's working, what isn't, how they feel, what they're learning, what needs changing.

Don't dump everything else. Portfolios must complement, not replace, the existing instructional program. Don't throw out something that's working. Keep what is good and fit portfolios into your existing curriculum as they meet a need.

Keep learning about portfolios. Changes in assessment are happening fast. More is being learned about portfolios daily. Keep on top of what's happening. Read books and articles, go to workshops, and visit classrooms where portfolios are being used. Once you start using portfolios, you'll need to keep learning about them more than ever.

Beware ready-made plans, programs, forms. All kinds of commercial organizations and publishers are getting on the portfolio bandwagon. Ready-made systems, plans and forms, whether purchased commercially or borrowed from another portfolio project, may give you good ideas. But you cannot take someone else's portfolio system and automatically transplant it into your classroom. The procedures and forms you develop or adapt yourself, with the help of your students, will always be the ones that work best.

Avoid the "holy grail" mentality. Portfolios may be wonderful, but they aren't the holy grail. They are not the only kind of assessment and they don't fix everything. Know what to expect from the portfolio process, and don't ask more of it than it can reasonably do.

Celebrate often. As you go along in the process, take time to recognize and enjoy accomplishments and growth. There is great joy in noticing growth, change, problems solved, learners blossoming. Celebrations—small or big, draw attention to the growth. They remind you of why you're doing portfolios to begin with.

A Portfolio may not be the pot of gold at the end of the rainbow... but it's the next best thing!

WRITING INVENTORY

How do you feel about writing? _____

What do you like to write about? _____

_____

Where and when do you like to write best? _____

_____

When you write, what is hardest for you to do? _____

_____

When you write, what do you do best? _____

_____

Do you think of yourself as a writer?   Why or Why not?

_____

What helps you with your writing? _____

_____

What makes a writer good? _____

_____

REFLECTING ON MY WRITING

Name_____ Date_____

Title of Writing_____

I chose this because_____

_____

_____

_____

_____

This shows that I'm good at_____

_____

_____

Next time, I'd like to try _____

_____

_____

write about it

SELF-REFLECTION

Name_____ Date_____

Title of Writing_____

I selected this as_____

because_____

_____

_____

_____

The strengths this shows are _____

_____

_____

_____

Something I need to work on or would like to try is ____

_____

_____

_____

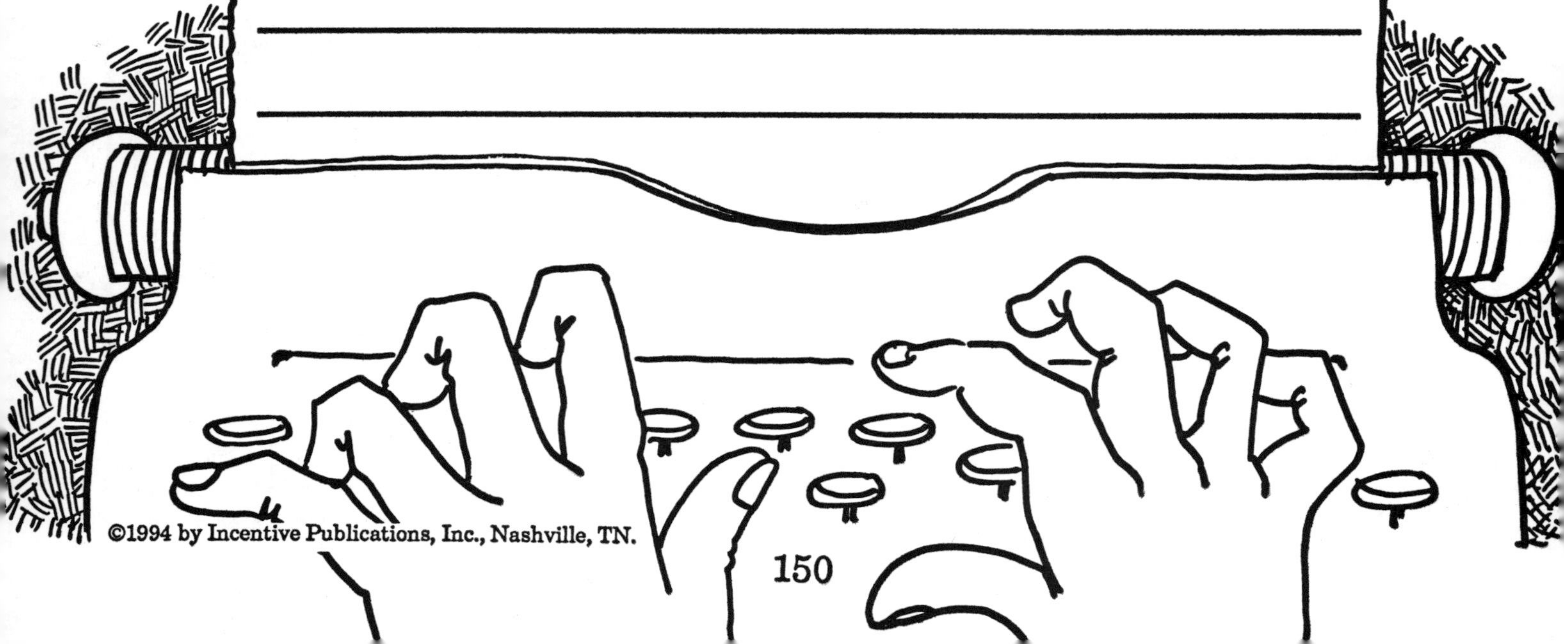

PEER REFLECTION

My name_____ Portfolio Owner_____ Date____

My favorite part of your portfolio is _____

because_____

_____

I notice that you're good at _____

_____

I think your best piece of writing is _____

because_____

_____

_____

Something I learned from you is _____

_____

_____
Signature

PARENT RESPONSE TO WRITING PORTFOLIO

Dear Parent(s)...

Thank you for joining in on the sharing of my Writing Portfolio. Please write your thoughts about the portfolio.
****

What was your favorite part of the portfolio?

Did anything in the portfolio surprise you?

What did you learn about my writing from the portfolio?

Compliments and comments:

*** **********

_____
Signature

ANECDOTAL NOTES....WRITING and WRITING PORTFOLIOS

Student _____   **Grade** _____

Date	Writing Piece or Process	Observations

WRITING PORTFOLIO REVIEW

Student   Teacher   Date

PORTFOLIO CONTENTS

STRENGTHS and NEEDS

SELF-REFLECTIONS

TEACHING POINTS

★

★

GOALS

★

★

WRITING PORTFOLIO CONFERENCE RECORD

Student

DATE	PORTFOLIO ELEMENTS	STRENGTHS & NEEDS	SELF–ANALYSIS	STUDENT COMMENTS	GOALS	COMMENTS

GUIDE FOR YOUR
METACOGNITIVE PORTFOLIO LETTER

Think about these questions:

- **What is the best thing about keeping a Writing Portfolio?**

- **What is the worst thing?**

- **What does the portfolio show about you as a writer?**

- **How did keeping a Writing Portfolio change you?**

- **Has anything good happened to you in keeping a portfolio?**

- **Has your attitude toward writing changed? How?**

- **What do you think about yourself as a writer?**

- **What do specific pieces of writing show about your growth?**

- **What have been your greatest improvements?**

- **Where do you want to go next with your writing?**

- **What would you do differently with your portfolio?**

Write a metacognitive letter to the teacher about your Writing Portfolio. Include the answers to some of these questions.

WRITING PORTFOLIO EVALUATION

Portfolio Owner

	PEER			SELF		
	YES	NO	SOME-WHAT	YES	NO	SOME-WHAT
The portfolio is well organized. I can find things in it easily.						
It has a clear Table of Contents.						
There is a good variety of kinds of writing.						
The portfolio includes a good number of samples.						
I can easily tell the purpose of the portfolio.						
There are serious, thoughtful self–reflections.						
The writing uses a variety of writing skills and traits.						
There are strong, readable individual pieces.						
I can see things that show me how the writer uses the writing process.						
I can learn something about the author from this portfolio.						
The portfolio is appealing and attractive.						
From looking at this portfolio, I can tell that its owner is really proud of it and very involved.						

_____   _____
Signature of Owner   *date*

_____   _____
Signature of Peer Reviewer   *date*

157

WRITING PORTFOLIO EVALUATION

Student

Date	Variety and Quantity of Writing	Use of Writing Traits and Skills	Use of Writing Process	Evidence of Writing Growth	Self–Evaluation	Use of Portfolio Processes	Personal Involvement and Attitude

WRITER'S STRENGTHS	WRITER'S WEAKNESSES / NEEDS	COMMENTS

CLASS PROFILE—WRITING PORTFOLIO PROGRESS & NEEDS

Teacher   **School Year**   **Date**

Student	Variety and Quantity of Writing	Use of Writing Traits and Skills	Use of Writing Process	Evidence of Writing Growth	Self-Evaluation	Use of Portfolio Processes	Personal Involvement and Attitude

OK = Acceptable   N = Needs Instruction   + = Outstanding